BOB SKELTON

I0569467

THE
AMAZING
POWER OF AN ENCOURAGER

The Tongue; The Most Powerful Tool
On The Planet

Does Yours Build Up Or Tear Down

THE AMAZING POWER OF AN ENCOURAGER:
The Tongue; The Most Powerful Tool On The Planet
Does Yours Build Up Or Tear Down

Copyright © 2025 Bob Skelton

ISBN (Paperback): 979-8-89672-023-2
ISBN (Ebook): 979-8-89672-024-9

All rights reserved. No part of this book may be used or reproduced by any means, graphic, electronic, or mechanical, including photocopying, recording, taping or by information storage and retrieval system without the written permission of the author except in the case of brief quotations embodied in critical articles and reviews.

Because of the dynamic nature of the Internet, any web addresses or links contained in this book may have changed since publication and may no longer be valid. The views expressed in the work are solely those of the author and do not necessarily reflect the views of the publisher, and the publisher hereby disclaims any responsibility for them.

Unless otherwise indicated, Scripture quotations taken from the New King James Version (NKJV). Copyright © 1982 by Thomas Nelson, Inc. Used by permission. All rights reserved.

Printed in the United States of America.

PROMINENT
BOOKS

5830 E 2nd St, Ste 7000 #9983
Casper, WY 82609
USA

CONTENTS

BOOK REVIEWS

Bob has been a friend for twenty years or more. He has run many things by me over the years for my advice. We have also flown many miles together in his plane across America as I was doing autograph sessions. I have been able to learn his passion for this country and the division that exists. He has shared his time with me; now it's my turn to tell you about my friend and our concern for this country. This book on encouragement is the key to building up people instead of tearing them down, and that will create an environment for Americans to unite. If we do not come together, this country cannot and will not stand as a free nation. Join us as we fight. We can never give up. As Bob says in his book, "When we are so divided, nothing else really matters." Look around. I agree!

—*Cale Yarborough*
3 TimeNASCAR Champion

This is a book all about change; change that is imperative to growth. This is not a book to be read. It is one to be absorbed, and if you give it the opportunity, it will make each and every one of you better...and who doesn't want that?!

—André Bauer
87th Lt. Governor of South Carolina

Bob, you originally conceived the book, "The Amazing Power Of An Encourager" for America, but as an international missionary, I can quickly say it is for the whole world because everyone—everywhere and every day—needs encouragement in what they do. This certainly energizes them to do that and more, still assuming they're doing it for the lifting up of all humanity. As you say, it will make you a better you.

—Jennifer Favour
International Missionary from Uganda

THE AMAZING POWER OF AN ENCOURAGER

WINNING AMERICA
WA
ENCOURAGE BUILDUP UNITE

The Amazing Power of an Encourager

Little Things Can Make a Big Difference

Be an ENCOURAGER

Vertical Encouragement

Horizontal Encouragement

The Sign is a Hook
To help sustain the message
For Encouragers

ACKNOWLEDGMENTS

I want to start by thanking my wife, Sue, by dedicating this book to her. We have been married since 1974. That was the best decision I have ever made, second only to my trusting Christ. Her encouragement during the darkest time in the life of our family was, without a doubt, the thing that changed the destiny of our family.

To my son, Grant; daughter-in-law, Rebecca; and the grandchildren, Harrison, Suzanne, and Adelle; Cale Yarborough; André Bauer; and Jennifer Favour, I want to express my gratitude for their support and encouragement in the development of this project. I know it is unusual to thank people who were negative toward your efforts, but I believe they have been used to help me sort out the fact that the need is greater than I thought, so thanks for the confirmation. It was the right thing to do.

HOPE
For America Tour

FOREWORD

A life without passion is a life that will never reach its God-given potential. Passion gives us purpose, drive, and a genuine desire to lead a life that makes a difference. Bob Skelton has passion! I have known Bob for more than 15 years. Our friendship began with a passion we both share: flying. Flying a plane is not for the faint of heart. It takes extreme dedication, concentration, and a complete confidence in your personal knowledge and skills. Bob and I both liked how it challenged our every sense and kept us mentally stimulated.

In 2002, after serving in the House of Representatives and then as a senator, I was elected as the 87th Lieutenant Governor of South Carolina. I was the youngest Lt. Governor in the country for eight years. I was driven by a passion to make a difference. I believe people could see this in me and responded to it. I wanted less government and more personal responsibility. If we could only instill passion back into our communities, we could truly make changes that would be everlasting. I was able to accomplish many things I am proud of during my years in office, but I was, at times, misunderstood. Some thought I wanted to stop the government from helping people in times of need. That was simply not the case; I wanted to empower our communities and help them find their passion, which would then make their need for government less. I worried greatly about our future generations and leaders. What would happen if everyone lost their drive and simply relied on the government? My time in office, gives me an innate ability to understand Bob. I believe he, too, is sometimes misunderstood, as is often the case with people with passion. Bob recognizes that our communities and our nation's future will be directly shaped by the youth of today. Their values, work ethic, and priorities will have profound impacts.

I hope you, too, can feel Bob's passion. This is a book all about change; change that is imperative to growth. This is not a book to be read. It is one to be absorbed, and if you give it the opportunity, it will make each and every one of you better...and who doesn't want that?!

—André Bauer
87th Lt. Governor of South Carolina

LETTER TO THE READER

Now, if there is one thing I know about my dad, outside of this new passion in his life, it is that he loves a challenge and is willing to do whatever it takes to see a task through to the end. I have never seen someone with a work ethic equal to his. When he told me was going to write a book, I was not as encouraging as I should have been. I was one of the first to point out, "Dad, you've never written a book!" That was no hindrance to him! This is a man who sets goals and does everything in his might to achieve them. I watched him use goal setting to build a successful business. I saw him set goals to develop as a pilot, which allowed me the amazing experience of growing up in planes flying all over the country. He even used goal setting to start playing golf at 61 years old. I truly don't think he was looking for a new way to spend his leisure time! I think he liked the challenge of the difficult sport. He awoke every morning to go to the driving range. He took lessons, watched instructional videos, read books, and hit thousands of balls! The whole time, he was setting goals to improve his swing, his drive distance, lower his putts, etc. Believe it or not, he became a pretty good golfer! Then it came to this new phase in his life: the writing of "The Amazing Power of An Encourager." I have again seen my dad use goal setting, determination, and passion to complete this new project. My desire is that you will read this book and join my dad. Join him in one of the greatest challenges of our time; the challenge to encourage a discouraged, divided nation. I ask you to join him and to experience "The Amazing Power of the Encourager."

—*Robert Grant Skelton*

A NOTE FROM ONE
OF THE EDITORS

Editing for Bob has opened my eyes to the different ways in which we can encourage others, even total strangers, in our daily lives. All in all, this powerful book has the potential to touch every generation and people of all backgrounds. In fact, if someone reads this book and doesn't have several "aha moments," then there is definitely a problem because reading it opens up the fact that it is possible to positively change the world through encouragement.

Dawn "D.A." Goodwin

Dawn "D.A." Goodwin earned a bachelor's degree in Political Science with a minor in English Language and Writing and, years later, she went on to earn a master's degree in English and Creative Writing so she could focus on bringing her passions for writing and editing to life. She is currently seeking a PhD in Education, and she teaches English Composition at a local college. Today Dawn also runs youreditingpro.net, a website that has been offering professional editing services since 2013. In addition, she edits books for other authors and is the editor of Diversity Works Magazine©.

The Offender I Once Defended is Dawn's first memoir, published under her pen name, D.A. Goodwin.

INTRODUCTION

When I was looking for a book title, I came up with several names. Then it seemed hard to decide which adjective would best describe the power of an encourager. I had phrases suggested to me like "the ultimate power," "the unmeasurable power," "the incredible power," and "the amazing ability of an encourager." In search of the most inspiring word to describe the word "power," I settled on "amazing."

During Thomas Edison's early school years, his teachers said he was stupid. His mother challenged the teachers. When she was ignored, Edison's mother chose to remove him from school. By removing Thomas from school and teaching him at home, history was changed forever. We might not have had the light bulb or any other of the 1,096 patented inventions had Edison's mother not taken an active role in directly encouraging and teaching young Thomas.

I have learned through my research that other people's opinions of you cannot define who you are, unless you let them. "No one knows your potential but God Himself."

Throughout history, there have been other powerful encouragers like Sir Winston Churchill, who served during Great Britain's darkest hour. One of his most important roles as British Prime Minister was to encourage the people not to surrender and to never, never, never give up. Sir Winston Churchill's encouragement changed the history of Great Britain, as well as the rest of the free world.

I can remember when the darkest days visited my family, and we lost everything. My wife could have destroyed me through discouragement, but Sue chose to encourage me instead. We worked long and hard to overcome our challenges, and Sue's encouragement to me was crucial to our positive recovery.

The Power of an Encourager™ is designed to challenge you, to inspire you, and ultimately, to encourage you. I want you to personally experience the positive feelings of encouragement and proactively explore new ways as to how you can spread the same feeling everywhere you go.

I believe, as you do, you will see the course of America change. As we lead the effort to encourage our fellow Americans, I believe we will also encourage our friends around the world, which has the potential to have a global impact. We simply need to make a choice to give encouragement a chance, just like Thomas Edison's mother did.

Most Americans have lost hope that our country will ever return to our founding fathers' values. America is divided in almost every way: politically, racially, and even in the church, which is the one place where unity should be modeled.

According to the American Foundation for Suicide Prevention, "Over 47,000 people committed suicide in 2017, 129 per day or 1 every 11 minutes, as well as 1.4 million attempted suicides." That number is rising every year, and trends indicate the suicide rate is growing more frequent among young people.[1] Could encouragement have made a difference in any of these cases?

I have absolutely no doubt, this could have had profound impact in many cases. It would be worth the time spent if only for one person. When I consider the people we pass every day, I wonder how many are hurting. Some statistics I've seen indicate eight out of ten people every day are dealing with some challenge; we call it life. The other two people out of ten will be dealing with something in their lives very soon. The point is so simple. Everyone needs encouragement. Will you be there?

Eddie Cantor said, "When I see the FBI's Top Ten Most Wanted list, I always think to myself, *If we'd made them feel wanted earlier, they wouldn't be wanted now.*"[2]

Can you encourage the wrong person? I don't think so, but if you do, we will forgive you. I'm convinced encouragement can change everything for most people.

I believe if you are a business owner, encouraging your stakeholders can change your company. Talk about a win-win scenario. Encouraging your employees will transfer to your vendors, customers, and leaders; serving each of them will make your business better.

Building the people, not the company.

"The Amazing Power of an Encourager" will change a country by bringing unity; racially, politically, and in the church. The secret to change is to get started.

William James said, "If you want to change your life for the better, you must start immediately, and do it flamboyantly."[3] I want to enlist you into our Army of Encouragers. The fuel that sustains encouragement is persistence. Encouragement is also the fuel for hope, which Americans need desperately.

This book is written to encourage my fellow Americans. Millions of dollars are being spent to divide this great nation by nefarious characters who profit from pitting one group of citizens against another. This division is destroying our nation and, if left unchecked, can and will destroy a family, a company, and even a country.

Throughout history, encouragement was the key in the darkest hours. If you love this country, on the next page I have a form asking you to commit to reading this book and trying the things I am suggesting. To chart a course change, we must be ready and willing to be a part of the correction.

That man in the mirror is the one person who can start a movement. One person who encourages another can start a movement that can, in turn, change America. To complete the effort, it will take millions, one at a time, to make the change permanent.

John Maxwell sums it up very nicely. Will you join me?

"I want to make a difference, *with people who want to make a difference,* doing something that makes a difference."[4]

—*John Maxwell*

COMMITMENT PAGE

The most important goals in life require a commitment. If you desire change for yourself, your family, and your country, are you willing to become an encourager? Will you commit a few minutes each day to putting into practice one or more of the ideas you learn in this book?

No commitment. No change.

Please commit to reading this book as fast as possible. Then commit to reading one chapter per day from Proverbs, and reread one chapter from *The Amazing Power of an Encourager* for one year to make this a part of your life. This will make you a better "you." (Change is slow and must be repeated so it becomes you.) "It's all about change."

Make this simple commitment to the person in the mirror. Just write down today's date, and sign your name.

Start Date __/__/____ Signature _____ As you begin to take action, please share your progress by posting your stories of giving or receiving encouragement on one of our websites:

BOB SKELTON

www.winningamerica.us
www.winningamerica.co
bob@winningamerica.us

*I challenge you to mentor someone. It will help you stay with the
program, and you will learn more as a result. Who is your person?*

----

*Does it make sense to you? If you can help someone
be better, and you want to do that, why not?*
"We can change the course of events if we
go to our knees in believing prayer."

—*Billy Graham*

CHAPTER ONE

Power of an Encourager™

WHEN YOU HEAR the word "power," what comes to your mind? In your mind's eye, do you see something positive or negative? When I think of the word "power," the immense forces of destruction, like the mushroom cloud of a nuclear weapon, come to mind. The tremendous power generated by an atom bomb is hard to fathom. When this weapon was first tested, the amount of energy it released was equal to twenty thousand tons of dynamite. The initial hydrogen bomb test unleashed energy equal to ten million tons of dynamite. How can our minds even understand what that means? A thermonuclear explosive weighing 2,400 pounds can release the same amount of energy equal to more than 1.2 million tons of TNT, which could level an entire metropolitan city. That is absolutely immense destructive power. Have you ever lived in an area impacted by raging forest fires? In 2018, *The New York Times* reported that California's tragic, record-breaking fire season destroyed 820,000 acres across the state; more than twice the area that burned at the same point the previous year.[5] Have you seen pictures of neighborhoods where charred home foundations are all that remain?

Consider for a moment just how devastating these powerful forces can be. On the other hand, the same explosive power of splitting atoms and burning fires can be harnessed to serve mankind. Nuclear plants provide clean electricity that can power thousands of homes, factories, and schools. Out of control forest fires are terrible, but wood logs cut and placed in a confined fireplace can provide life-saving winter warmth.

Q: Can you think of another force that appears in nature and possesses both massive destructive *and* considerable constructive capabilities?

A: The power of the spoken word

A negative spoken word, especially when delivered by an authority figure, has as much destructive capability to destroy lives as a nuclear weapon. Conversely, when a strong leader shares a motivating word of encouragement, the recipient can be energized to move mountains.

History gives us examples of leaders of every stripe that have used words to lift people up or to beat people into submission and destroy lives. Think about the leaders that impact your life: pastors, teachers, politicians, business executives, parents, bosses, coaches; and even your physician.

Do we ever stop and consider how damaging an unkind word could be? Think about words spoken describing another human being such as, "He is a dud," or "He is a loser." Good teachers can see a student's potential in some ways, but God

Himself only knows anyone's full potential. I often hear stories about students who have been told they did not possess a certain ability. Then at some point in the future, a new teacher appears who speaks life and success through a few words of encouragement, leading the student to excel in the area that he or she was said to not have that ability.

Thomas Edison was told he was stupid, and Walt Disney was told he did not have imagination. Any further questions? Let's define the word "encourage." According to dictionary.com, it's a verb (used with object), **en·cour·aged, en·cour·ag·ing,** and its definition is: to stimulate by assistance, approval, etc.

His coach encouraged him throughout the marathon race to keep on running.

One of the chief duties of a teacher is to encourage students, to promote, advance, or foster: Poverty often encourages crime.[6]

Encouragement changed the destiny of my life for my family and me. When we nearly lost everything in a bad business decision after the economy bottomed out, my wife could have discouraged me. I could have made another attempt to take my life.

Sue never hounded me with the fact that it was my decision to pursue the unwise business venture she had specifically warned me not to go into. Even after selling everything we could to pay our debts, we still owed $90,000 at a 19.5 percent interest rate as a result of my unwise decision.

We started working smarter, not harder, and were able to retire the debt, and the next few years in the prosthetic business became very profitable. The impact of Sue's encouragement was evident in my success. After restructuring our company and paying off the $90,000, my income was four times more than

I had ever made in my life. The next year, it doubled again, and then again.

Without my wife's encouragement, I would have likely given up when I thought there was no hope for my family. Instead, my business prospered. We were able to send our son to college for an undergraduate and two master's degrees without any debt. We have been able to purchase two new homes, four airplanes, and a condo at the beach and live a debt-free, comfortable retirement. I don't share this to impress you. I share it to impress upon you *The Amazing Power of an Encourager*™. This also explains many of the problems America faces today.

We are so self-centered today; politically, racially, and even in the church. It seems that people are more interested in competing with their fellow man instead of lifting him or her up. Racial division is especially heinous and is one of the most destructive uses of the spoken word.

I have a friend who is a high school senior. His mom is white, and his dad is black. While on a church youth group trip one summer, they ran into a retired white baseball player. The kids were excited and asked him to take a picture with them. The player agreed until he noticed the black member of their group. Unbelievably, he stopped the proceedings and asked the black youth to step out of the picture; otherwise, he would not agree to take the photo. The young boy very kindly stepped out of view.

The baseball player hurt this impressionable young man, who is a top-notch individual. The white ballplayer is not a good role model for the kids, and, as it turns out, he has had all kinds of legal problems from gambling and other addictions. This young man's character is so much higher than the white ballplayer's. His friends rallied around to encourage him after the painful episode. Imagine if the ballplayer had used encouraging words that created unity and pride in being an American, regardless of color or creed.

Incidents like this should never happen. Human beings should not treat each other this way, but we do. Someone has to take the first step to unify by encouraging people and not discouraging them. Then, and only then will we see changes that can create a massive impact that begins with one word of encouragement.

At the end of every chapter there are questions to consider and a place to make notes.

CHAPTER TWO

People Are Hurting

EIGHT OUT OF *ten people you meet in any given day are hurting.* When I share this statement with people, the response I most frequently get is something like, "Really? I would guess it's higher—maybe nine out of ten." I had an appointment with my family physician this week, who has been a friend for a number of years. He asked what I was up to, now that I was no longer practicing. So I shared the book project, *The Amazing Power of an Encourager*™, and his comments were, "That is so needed. When we get with other physicians, we are always expressing the tremendous increase in depression in our practices."

Here's the bigger issue. When we feel pain, we have a desperate urge to unload it, and typically, the recipient is someone close to us. As I think back to the days when my business was getting hammered, I was hurting badly. No one really knew how bad it was except my wife. We did not talk to our friends or family about our business problems. We hide our pain and suffering pretty well, even from our closest friends, despite the fact that I was only sleeping a few hours a night.

How much do you know about the real circumstances in other people's lives? While their pain may not be traumatic or overtly apparent, you can imagine most people carry some chronic circumstances with them every single day. Many times, their biggest pain is rooted in the fear of the unknown, which can be fueled by multiple factors in their personal lives.

For example, the root cause of many pains can be division. When people do not feel as one with their family, peers, or community, the manifestation of that pain can be awful. People experience division at work, in politics, among races or genders, and even in our churches, where unity is supposed to be modeled.

This pain is easily extended to our direct family. What happens when children live in a home where mom and dad cannot get along? What about the pain of separation? What about in single-parent homes where the breadwinner is working two jobs to support the family and kids feel the crushing pain of loneliness or abandonment?

The share of U.S. children living with an unmarried parent has more than doubled since 1968, jumping from 13 percent to 32 percent in 2017. That trend has been accompanied by a drop in the share of children living with two married parents, down from 85 percent in 1968 to 65 percent. Some 3 percent of children are not living with any parents, according to a new Pew Research Center analysis of U.S. Census Bureau data.

Most children in unmarried parent households are living with a solo mother, but a growing share is living with cohabiting parents. Overall, about one in five children (21 percent) is living with a solo mother, up from 12 percent in 1968. Some

7 percent are living with cohabiting parents, about double the share that were doing so in 1997 (the first year for which census data on cohabitation is available). The share of children living with a solo father has ticked up and stands at 4 percent, up from 1 percent in 1968.

(In this analysis, children are classified based on the parent with whom they live most of the time. Children who split their time equally between households are classified based on which household they were in at the time of the data collection.) All told, 24 million U.S. children younger than 18 are living with an unmarried parent. Most (15 million) are living with a solo mother. In comparison, 5 million live with cohabiting parents, and 3 million live with a solo father. In 1968, the first year for which these data are publicly available, 9 million children were living with an unmarried parent, 8 million of whom had a solo mom.[7] Kids face more challenges when they grow up in insecure environments, which translates to more pain driven to the core of the family unit.

Consider the horrendous suicide rate. According to the American Foundation for Suicide Prevention (AFSP), the Centers for Disease Control and Prevention (CDC) reported that 47,176 Americans took their own lives in 2017, and 1.4 million attempted.[8] That's one hurting person dying every eleven minutes. How much pain does a person have to be carrying inside to kill himself or herself?

The AFSP says nine out of ten teens who commit suicide have been diagnosed with mental health issues, depression, or related issues.[9] How could an encouraging word or even a few minutes of sincere listening have reduced those numbers? The smallest gesture of kindness, like a kind smile, buying someone's lunch, or spending a few choice moments in conversation, can have a massive impact. What may first appear as a little thing can make a big difference to those needing encouragement.

An unknown person has written these words, "Hurting people hurt people." I really believe this is true. I read this story of a father and a son who were walking together in the woods, and they came upon an animal that had been caught in a hunter's trap. The animal was in obvious distress.

The son was moving toward the animal to free it when his father stopped him to explain, "Be careful. A hurt animal will bite the one closest, even someone who is trying to help him." What is true of animals is true of people. Hurting people hurt people. We've all seen parents under a lot of stress strike out at their children, maybe undeservingly.

While recently vacationing in Florida, as we were checking into the resort, we were briefed on a variety of property benefits. The concierge staff escorted us to different stations around the venue to explain all the features. During this tour, we were offered a bonus to sign up for a timeshare presentation. If we had backed out, we would have forfeited $20 and a world-class breakfast. Although we decided in advance we were not going to purchase a timeshare, no matter how amazing the sales pitch, we figured we might as well listen to the story and claim our cash and breakfast. As so often happens, although we didn't know why we should go, we felt sure it was exactly what we needed to do. It turns out, the opportunity to meet Marie, our sales associate, was the precise reason we needed to attend the presentation. (Marie is not her real name.) When Marie sat down and began the pre-sales pitch warm-up, her first question opened the door for me to describe the power of encouragement and explain why I was writing a book on the subject. Marie's countenance immediately changed as she became very transparent with us about her life.

This was a prime example of what happens when we give hurting people an opportunity to open up and share.

As she began to talk for a few minutes, we learned Marie is a single mom with two pre-teen children. Her marriage was a very abusive one, and her husband had been sent to prison for his abuse and was later deported to Colombia. This brief moment gave us a chance to get a better understanding of the deep-seated emotional pain of another human being. Sadly, this kind of deep pain is common in our society. People are hurting.

Marie is a young lady working hard to provide for her family. She is lonely for a companion and has important spiritual needs. Marie has attempted to seek friendships at a local church, but sadly, she was met by people with judgmental spirits regarding the reasons her husband was abusive. Marie went on to share how she'd been spending time with her co-workers at the bars, jumping from one unhealthy relationship to the next. It seems many of her colleagues were living hopeless lives as well.

We didn't do much but listen quietly and give Marie an opportunity to share her burden. Did our time on vacation change our desire to encourage someone that we had never met? We obviously had no idea we were going to meet Marie. My wife asked her for her contact information, so we could stay in touch and continue to encourage her. Marie agreed, and now we have had several occasions to continue the long-distance relation with her.

Marie has been so appreciative and thankful for our meeting (even though we didn't buy a timeshare). We may never see Marie again in person, but we can still make a difference in this lady's life and, by extension, the lives of her sweet children.

Marie was telling us a story about the wealthy owner of the timeshare company. He has money, but no peace. With a hopeless lifestyle, his daughter, who also worked for the company, decided to commit suicide in one of his properties. When we see people who are looking for peace and joy in things or the next party, as long as they are in the search, they still have hope in what those things will give them. It is not until they get those things that they realize the hopelessness in things and that it is not what they envisioned them to be. People are hurting because they have either lost hope in their pursuits or are losing hope at a fast pace. Hopelessness appears like a snowball going down a slope; the farther it rolls, the faster it goes, and the bigger it gets.

What could a few choice minutes of your time be worth to people rapidly approaching the hopeless point of no return? This is an open door for you to share the hope of Christ.

Look for someone you can invest a few minutes in today. Starting is always the hardest part. The time you give someone who is hurting can be worth more than you can ever imagine. Let me encourage you. Being an encourager will always do something for you. What follows are a number of insights I have learned from my personal story. Our mission is that we might challenge others to be encouragers. This book is simply intended for people who want to serve as an encouragement to make a difference in the lives of others by sharing hope when they are ready.

Please do not take anything I'm sharing as professional counseling.

If you need professional counseling, especially if you have been contemplating suicide, please get help now. I say this, not to weaken the power of encouragement, but to add credibility to these plans for change to become a better you.

Hopelessness is not confined to low-income families; quite the opposite. In *Mental Health Daily, Why Suicides Are More Common in Richer Neighborhoods*, I discovered this article by Daniel Wilson, senior economist at the San Francisco Federal Reserve, and two co-authors who compared individuals with the same income living in two different counties. The person living in the rural areas of a county with a higher than average income is 4.5 percent more likely to commit suicide.[10] At first glance, this might seem surprising, but it begins to make sense when you think about how we tend to compare ourselves to those around us. People are most driven to suicide when they view their current situation as completely hopeless with no possibility of creating a better future. Could an encouraging word help someone in this mindset? Absolutely. The number one thing contributing to suicide is relationship based; someone just being there to listen could be the difference. Other common causes of suicide include depression, drug abuse, financial problems, as well as difficulties with relationships. In spite of the availability of crisis hotlines, the jury is still out on their effectiveness.

If you choose to be an encourager, there are several important characteristics I've recognized in hurting people that I'd like to share with you. Most of the time, no matter what the person's tough exterior may appear to be, hurting people can have a very low self image. Frequently, deep down, they don't believe they deserve anyone's help.

What about people who are well known or famous? Can they live a normal life? Having owned four airplanes, Sue and I have found it's a lot like people you may know who own a boat or a pick-up truck. You always seem to have more friends, especially when they'd like to play with your toys. That can be a little intoxicating to the ego, but I got a glimpse into the prison and pain a lot of celebrities live in.

I have been blessed with the privilege of getting to know and fly some pretty well-known people. As we traveled together, frequently we were not able to eat in a public restaurant. It seemed that no matter where we were, my famous friends would take a couple bites of food and a well-meaning fan would recognize them. He or she would stop at the table and share a well-intended word of praise or appreciation. However, at the end of the day, most fans seemed clueless that this is a real person who would like to enjoy a meal in peace. By the time the visit was over, the meal would be cold. This is not a pleasurable time for well-known people. For most of us, we can go out with friends, relax and enjoy a good meal. For them, without booking a private dining room in a high-end restaurant, good conversation is nearly impossible. They stop going out and spend more and more time alone, which can lead to a very lonely private life.

I was meeting with a friend who happens to be a former state governor. As I was leaving his office, he said, "Bob, let me tell you something about celebrities. They are all very lonely people."

If you genuinely want to be an encourager, it is very possible you need to reach out to someone who may be a well-known person. It's easy to assume that the well-known person has lots of friends, but often times, they only have people around them who want something.

Many times, this includes people who are easily recognized in the community, maybe prominent doctors, business people, politicians, or community leaders. If a door opens through the course of your daily routine, you may be surprised about whom you can connect with. You may be even more surprised when you discover how ready they are to have someone who will simply be a friend with an open ear.

As you develop these types of relationships using *The Amazing Power of an Encourager*™, realize that you will likely learn things about people that should be kept confidential. What you'll discover is that when you become a great listener, which often happens by not filling silence with your own words, people will say things that amaze you.

You may be tempted to share what you learn with others, even when you have not been asked to keep a discussion confidential. However, presume that everything you learn in private conversations is just for the two of you unless there is an agreement to share it. With high trust, the power of your words and actions create much stronger encouragement. As you develop these skills, you may be surprised at the quality of the friendly relationships you cultivate. You will also find many of these friends will become your greatest encouragers.

I have a couple of friends who are really close to me. Our relationships are grounded in trust. Trust is difficult to earn and easy to destroy, and trust is earned slowly. That's why I recommend you err on the side of privacy and not share anything unless given permission. This is why it takes time to build those kinds of relationships.

Just like a great barbecue that is slow cooked, these types of relationships are best developed over time because most hurting or lonely people don't know how to start a relationship or to maintain one. They have never had the opportunity to enjoy the kind of friendship and encouragement represented by someone who truly cares for them. Frequently, these people are extremely slow to let their guard down until you have their trust.

When you have their trust, guard it like Fort Knox, or you can lose it in no time flat. For the encourager, these hurting people can be the hardest ones to deal with, but these relationships can be incredibly rewarding.

A friend of mind was doing a workshop in Charlotte, North Carolina. At the end of the class, a gentleman came up to him and said he wanted the book that the speaker had referred to during the workshop. The book was called *Happiness Is a Choice.* The gentleman told the speaker, "I want that book!" He went on to say, "I can buy anyone in this room; I can buy you. I want that book." So the speaker proceeded to hand the gentleman the book, but did not let go of it until the gentleman promised to bring it back the next week, which he agreed to do.

One week later, my friend returned to deliver his workshop, and the gentleman came in an hour earlier. The man said, "I need to talk to you. Last week when I left here and went home, I did not lay this book down until I had read everything you had underlined. Then I went back and read everything between the markings. Then I put the book down, picked up my pistol, and emptied the chamber of the bullets I had intended to use to kill myself."

Happiness is a choice. It is never hopeless unless we give up. Giving up is not a good option. If the gentleman in the above story had given up, life would have been so much more different for the people he said he loved. Suicide is the most selfish act because, in the end, it's all about you. Sadly though, we all know every story doesn't turn out that way.

Those who claim to be religious people have been known for their cruelty to those who are not like them. We know it's true; hurting people hurt people. For those who read the Bible, we come to the words of Jesus: "But I say to you who hear, Love your enemies, do good to those who hate you, bless those who curse you, and pray for those who spitefully use you." (*New King James Version Bible,* Luke 6:27-28)

Why do we find it so hard to live like that? Why do we feel the need to strike out at others, whether they are our children, spouse, neighbor, another race, or someone whose lifestyle is deplorable by our standards? Why can't we live and let live? Why do we have to utter hurtful words to or about any other human being? And why do other people, sometimes those closest to us, turn on us and say such hurtful things? Again, this simple phrase has the answer as to why: hurting people hurt people. People who hurt others and us may themselves have hurts that are causing them to act out in ways that they never would have otherwise acted. When we encounter someone who is lashing out at other people, we need to ask: *What could be going on in his or her life that is causing him or her to behave this way?*

A professor tells about a scathing letter he received at a college where he once served. The first few lines were demoralizing. After reading a few paragraphs, he skipped to the end of the letter to see who the writer was. He did not recognize the signer, so he phoned the registrar and asked him to bring the folder of the student whose name was on the letter. The registrar walked in a few minutes later with the folder and had the flap of it pulled back to reveal the picture of the young lady who had written the letter. He recognized her at once, and his feelings of defensiveness against her harsh letter melted into understanding.

She was a beautiful young woman who had suffered a diving accident the previous year at summer camp. She was paralyzed from her neck down. Although the state paid the bill, and the college, including students, did all it could to help her, she was unable to accept herself after the accident. She lashed out at the people who pushed her wheelchair. She was angry with everyone and bitter.

The young woman's letter to the professor addressed his insensitivity to her needs on campus. His momentary spirit of anger eased into a mellowness as he said to himself, *I really don't know what my attitude might be if I were forced to cope with the same kinds of physical problems that she has to cope with.*

This is like an angry driver who screams at us in traffic, the impatient police officer who pulls us over refusing to listen to our explanation, or the spouse who is constantly belittling us. In each case, that person may have things going on in his or her life that are causing great distress. Whenever anyone lashes out at us with hurting words or attitudes, rather than striking back, we need to ask ourselves what could be causing him or her to act out such anger that way. Sometimes we can defuse the situation by a quiet comment like, "It must be very stressful having to deal with what you deal with all day."

Hurting people hurt people. When you are hurting, you need to think about how it might affect others. You can easily hurt others when you are hurting. There is a term many psychiatrists use today, which is "LFT." This abbreviated term addresses a prevalent problem in our society. LFT stands for "Low Frustration Tolerance." This is when we let our emotions cause us to respond in ways that are not normal, and sometimes even dangerous, for us. Many Americans are walking time bombs, just waiting to explode. Let me give you an example; road rage when someone cuts in front of you. Then you start to drive crazy, making unwise moves in your car to let the person know how unhappy you are with his or her action. This kind of behavior is getting more and more common.

We all allow circumstances, situations, schedules, and people to crowd out our ability to tolerate frustrations. For this reason, so many of us live on the edge and erupt with anger when frustrations arise. This is Low Frustration Tolerance when it shows its ugly head. It doesn't take much to set most of us off, especially when we are tired or stressed and feeling down on ourselves. Like the animal in the hunter's trap, we feel vulnerable. We need to examine ourselves and ask if we are acting appropriately. We can cause untold damage to those around us, especially those we love—those we depend on.

An encourager will model patience, always wanting to leave others better than we found them. When we leave them, we should leave them better, not worse. I might repeat this several times throughout the book because this book is really all about change.

QUESTIONS TO CONSIDER

1. *What would you like to change to become a better you?*

2. *When do you have moments of LFT? With family?*

3. *Who are you investing time in to be an encourager? (Start with your family) 1._____ 2._____ 3._____*

4. *If you learn to control your frustration tolerance level, would it make you a better you?*

5. *Would you have more influence with the people you come in contact with every day if you had control of LFT?*

CHAPTER THREE

Three Types of People Who Come Into Our Presence Every Day

IN THIS CHAPTER, I will give you my best insight based on my extensive experience in dealing with people in personal and professional settings. I'm specifically using a visual metaphor of a traffic signal with red, yellow, and green lights to give you a way to think about how you interact with people who come into your presence every day.

Please keep in mind, I am not passing judgment on these people but rather focusing on these personality styles as they relate to your work as an encourager. These illustrations resonate with people. Whether I'm speaking to a group or sharing with them on an individual basis, people agree with these observations, and often, they begin to recall their associates who fit in one of the three categories.

RED LIGHT

This is not the person you want to aspire to be. These individuals drain you and everyone they come in contact with emotionally. People dread to see them. When they are in your presence for more than a couple of minutes, they zap all the energy from you emotionally and you soon lose your excitement. Sometimes this person does not have to come into your physical presence; they can have this effect by writing a letter or making a social media post.

I was talking to my pastor one day using this illustration, and a specific person immediately came to his mind. This person writes him constantly without a single kind or encouraging word. Whenever these types of people are discussing others, the nature of the conversation always leads to a gossip-style assault on another person's character. Their opinions are always the "right" ones, and nobody else can compete.

It doesn't matter what you might suggest; they always have the best answers. Everything in their life revolves around themselves. Most of the time, this personality style indicates a low self-image, which suggests much deeper psychological issues.

One of the most astonishing characteristics of these types of people is that they think when they come into your presence, they brighten your life. They may actually be one of the most intelligent people on the face of the earth you know. They are well read, but the only person they really impress is themselves.

They are clueless about their effect on others and have no idea of the emotional drain they have on other people. They can kill a person's desire or bridle his or her excitement. When they leave, you are thrilled to say goodbye, so you can go take a shower and a nap.

This profile can also become apparent on the public stage when they are speaking publicly to a group. Frequently, on a platform, they will make statements as a subject matter expert, but when you challenge their authority, they attack you. They frequently take legitimate questions about their topic as personal attacks, and they have very thin skin. This immediately shatters their own credibility. It often indicates they will make comments about you behind your back, questioning your character. Meeting with them one-on-one is likely going to take all the wind from your sails. You are more likely to be completely discouraged and worse off.

They do not realize how much of a discourager they are most of the time. This is especially true when they do not get the desired results from their own performance. Their tendency is to blame someone or something else, and they do not take responsibility for their actions.

I remember attending a meeting where the speaker did not get the response he felt he should have received. He threw his book down and stormed out of the room. His audience was made to feel like he was the immature little boy. *If you don't play the way I want you to play, I will take my toys and go home.* This kind of behavior will destroy an encourager. Unfortunately, this behavior is modeled way too much in public and creates more unnecessary division. Public speakers sometimes encourage from the platform and remove it when you talk to them one on one.

If you look in the mirror and see this type of behavior, here's the good news. You are the only one who can decide to change. This may be a tough pill to swallow, but better now than never. You can attack me if you like, but deep down, you know I'm right. Put down your inner "attack dog," and let the rest of this book encourage you. You can change, and when you do, your life can be amazing.

YELLOW LIGHT

The easiest way to describe this person is lukewarm. There are many people in this category. You know these folks because when they come into your presence, they don't bring anything to the party, and they don't take anything away unless they stay too long. Why does it seem easy to be like this person? They can be described as unmotivated. They are often intelligent, but they do not seem to have any interest in applying their capabilities to do anything productive. They seem bored and they bore others. They engage in mindless activities and do not put any effort forth to serve others or productively enrich themselves. Why does this person not bring value to himself or others? I believe they have yet to find their purpose in life. You can't give what you don't have. You can't share what you don't know. These people allow their television, the Internet, or social media to tell them what to think and believe.

Sometimes these people can be the worst source on earth for information and for help in forming values. Unless you have discernment about the influential information sources that drive what you believe, you can easily be driven into a purposeless existence.

The reality is that letting someone else think for you is easy. It doesn't take any effort, and if you are not motivated to read or study, then you reap what you sow. This often manifests itself in accepting minimum performance jobs that simply drive an existence, not an exciting life. Unfortunately for those who choose this lifestyle, what appears to be an easy choice leads to an empty wagon down life's road. The impact of this person's choice on others is profound. It is nearly impossible for them to encourage others.

If there were a scientific way to measure red, yellow, and green, my guess is that yellow is probably the largest group of people. I decided to write this book to create an awareness and challenge people to make a change, but of course, that ultimately depends upon you. Statistically speaking, it's likely you may fall into the yellow category. If so, please see this as a great day. You can decide to warm up, take on life with vigor, and put your God-given gifts to work for you and others. I hope you find these words encouraging because I believe in you and can't wait to see what a difference this makes for you. You can make a difference in your home, town, and nation, but starting is the hardest part. It's up to you. Are you in?

GREEN LIGHT

This is the person I have been waiting to describe since starting this chapter. Just thinking about this person brings a smile to my face. When he or she comes into your presence, it's like a breath of fresh air. This person brings a spirit of abundance and possibility, like a beautiful day when it is so clear that you can see for miles. Nature takes on vivid detail. You get the same personal experience like the thirst you have on a boiling hot summer afternoon up until the moment you experience the satisfying cool drink of water from a mountain spring that quenches your parched throat. *Does someone like the person I've just described come to mind?*

Do you begin to smile, like I do, when this person comes into your presence because you know he or she is bringing encouragement? Every minute you spend with him or her is refreshing, stimulating and so empowering. The encourager type of person begins to inspire you to start thinking that the impossible could very well be possible. If you are having a cloudy day, as soon as your interaction begins, the dark clouds begin to dissipate, being replaced by blue skies. This person embodies the proverb that "laughter is like good medicine." He or she always brings good cheer.

This person also gives us a prime example that life is short, and we should enjoy every moment to its fullest. He or she always bring something valuable to your conversation, whether it's a long face-to-face meeting, a brief telephone discussion, or an interaction online on a social media platform. The bottom line is, the encourager always leaves you better than he or she found you.

We have described three different kinds of people who come into our presence every day. When you look in the mirror most of the time, do you see red, yellow, or green? The truth is, depending on the day, sometimes we have characteristics of all three. Who we are most often has a big impact on every life we touch. Depending on our own attitudes and how conscious we are about our impact on others, we can be tremendous, marginal, or negative encouragers. This is where we each have to put on our thick skin and take a hard look at ourselves. Being honest with yourself is one of most difficult, if not the most difficult, requirements for personal change. For instance, if you were told you had a life-threatening disease, your life would depend on receiving the proper medical diagnosis. Most of us might not realize we have dirt on our face until we look into the mirror. It will take a conscious effort on your part to reach a proper conclusion about your impact on others.

The key is to take responsibility for who you are and become a better you. This book is to serve you and encourage you to make changes to improve your life and every life you touch. One person can correct the course of our country because what starts with one multiplies exponentially.

I will be the first to admit, it will be some of the hardest work you've ever done. I know because I've gone through the humbling process myself. When we accept ourselves as God made us and not try to be someone else, we will not be frustrated and unfulfilled. I need to realize that no one knows my potential—only God—and then I must strive to be the best me. There is still a lot of change needed to make me a better me. That starts with me taking the focus off of me and putting it on others. This will get you where most of the world is striving to get—fame, fortune, joy—but in a different way, and when you get there, it is fulfilling, not disappointing, and will last the rest of your life.

Our nation, for the most part, is all about me, my family, and no more. For our nation to have a course correction, it will have to happen to millions, one at a time, and no one can do your part; only you. As I have traveled across America, it has seemed that everyone wants change, but no one thinks it is him or her who needs to change. Secondly, if a person agrees it is he or she, that individual will not pay the price for change. To know is nothing; to do is everything. It's your decision and mine to be an encourager or not.

QUESTIONS TO CONSIDER

1. Which one of the three personality types—red, yellow, or green—best describes you? Why?

2. Share this chapter with three friends and ask them to write you anonymously tell you if you are red, yellow, or green. (you must explain what the three are)

3. Is there a difference between your self-assessment and your friends' observations? Why do you think that is?

4. Which personality areas do you think are most important for you to improve?

5. What is your plan to improve in these areas?

6. How will you sustain the change, and to whom will you be accountable?

7. Imagine six months into the future.

8. What will be the effect of your daily decision to change?

9. Explain how the new "you" has impacted your life and those around you.

Always Remember

We also go into the presence of others every day and when we do, how should we leave them?

There are three choices. One: we can leave them *better*. Two: we can leave them the *same*. Three: we can leave them *worse*. The correct answer is to always leave them better!

CHAPTER FOUR

What Being an Encourager Does for You

WHAT WILL THE process of becoming an avid encourager do for you? Good question. First, you must realize the decision to encourage others starts a process of change within you. The prevailing question most people ask is, *What's in it for me?* As you begin looking for ways to encourage others, you will start to ask a different question: *What's in it for them?*

The opportunities to encourage others will begin to appear as soon as you begin to actively look for ways to encourage others. At the same time, almost as a byproduct, your influence will broaden. You will start to see positive things happen in your life that you cannot explain. As this starts to happen, if you are like me, you'll realize this is much bigger than you, which requires relying on what I call "Vertical Encouragement."

As a Christian, I look to God to develop a relationship with Him through prayer and meditation on the Word to understand the mind of God. This is the practical, vertical encouragement that recharges my battery by reading God's Word, the Bible. About thirty years ago, I started reading the book of Proverbs. One of the great things about this powerful book is that there are thirty-one chapters, one for every day of the month. For the horizontal relationship, read one chapter a day from *The Amazing Power of an Encourager* one chapter from the Proverbs. This is for our relationship with each other.

Muhtar Kent, who was Chairman of the Board of Directors of the Coca-Cola Company, says, "Every time I visit a college campus or speak with young professionals one on one, I am inevitably asked, "What single attribute do you think is most accountable for your success in business? I tell them, without hesitation, that I never dine alone."

Every moment of every day is an opportunity to start or strengthen a relationship, and those relationships, if cultivated, can lead to incredible opportunities for everyone involved. For me, relationships are the single-most important element I bring to my role as Chairman and CEO of The Coca-Cola Company. Quite frankly, they are what got me here. And the biggest lesson I've learned over the years regarding relationships is that they only work when you're there for people during the good and bad times. Similar to marriage vows, those ancient words are etched in wisdom.[11] Although this man has had extreme demands on his time, he understands the crucial importance of building relationships.

An encourager needs to be a person of influence. To be a person of influence requires having good relationships with people, especially those you wish to encourage. Sometimes relationships can develop quickly. In other cases, they can take years.

I know people who met one week and, three weeks later, they are getting married. Amazingly, they are still happily married decades later. Other folks, like my wife and I, took three years to get to know each other before walking down the aisle. In most cases, developing relationships takes time, so you need to be patient.

There are occasions when you may be called on to be an encourager without any advanced notice. I had an encourager share a story about an experience he had at work. A terrible workplace accident had just occurred, and his coworkers asked him to pray. With many injuries and even one death, people were traumatized. At the time, he didn't realize the impact of his prayerful encouragement.

Months later, he was shocked to learn how impactful his words had been. First responders, coworkers, and family members came to the encourager individually and let him know how hopeful his words of encouragement were in that painful moment. While it was hard for him to comprehend, his story confirmed what I've always believed; it's the little things that make the big difference. This is another example that anyone willing to be a giver of himself or herself can be an encourager. You are not required to have special talents to write like a poet or even speak like a news anchor to be effective. You may never know how encouraging you are to another person. Your brief moment of encouragement may be just the right words for a person struggling with an issue.

When you are predisposed to look for opportunities to encourage others, you are spreading joy without asking for anything in return. It's a selfless act. You can spread encouragement in a checkout line talking to another customer while you wait.

Think about times when you've been frustrated in a public place, waiting in line or dealing with a problem. Has anyone ever said something nice to you that took the edge off the situation? I know it's happened to me. In fact, there may be a circumstance where you see the red-light person we talked about in Chapter 3 giving someone else a hard time. If you can find an appropriate way to be the green light for the person in distress, you may help diffuse an unpleasant circumstance.

While this may not be easy to do at first, if you keep a keen eye out for ways to help, you may be surprised how many opportunities you have to encourage others. In situations where you are interacting with people you know, your encouragement to others will build your credibility. You will have demonstrated, in real time, what it looks like to serve others without expecting anything in return. This translates into the law of sowing and reaping. When you sow good seeds into the ground, you are much more likely to get a plentiful harvest. Not every seed will grow.

Some fall on bad soil. The birds eat some of them, but in the end, good seeds sown and watered with a good attitude will yield a nice crop.

An encourager needs to constantly challenge himself to grow. These scenarios are examples of when you can also miss your opportunity because you chose to sit on the sidelines and wait for someone else to step up and be the encourager. Don't wait. No situation is ever perfect. As you accept the challenge to become a better you, the byproduct of stepping up in uncertain times will make you more valuable.

QUESTIONS TO CONSIDER

1. We started this chapter asking what will the process of becoming an avid encourager do for you?

2. What are the two different kinds of relationships we need to develop in order to be an effective encourager?

3. Can a person be a good horizontal encourager without getting vertical encouragement?

4. What is important about relationships and encouragement?

PROGRESS REPORT

How do you like what being an encourager is doing for you?

Is it making you a better you? You need to ask you friends. (write their comments)

If you are not making progress, why? This book is all about change.

CHAPTER FIVE

What an Encourager Looks Like

H OW WOULD YOU *describe an encourager to someone who has been living in a cave, not interacting with people?*

If a person were to walk into a room of people, could you pick out which person was the encourager? What signs would you look for to help you select this standout person? Most of the time, encouragers will have a lot of people around them, but they will not be loud or the center of attention. Typically, you'll find they just appear as one of the people in a group. When they speak, they are usually asking great questions or trying to help. It seems like they know everyone, and frequently, they are beloved members of their community. Encouragers express concern for others, especially the underdog or the person with the greatest need. Another common trait is encouragers are always the same type of person, regardless of whether you meet them at a concert, in the workplace, at church, in the shopping mall, or at home. They are willing to invest time in people, not projects. In our society, where eight out of ten people you meet are hurting, encouragers make the time to help.

I recently watched an inspiring video about a package delivery driver. On her daily route, she was making deliveries and, at one stop, she helped a customer carry boxes to the doorstep. As the driver and customer were walking up the driveway, the homeowner asked the female driver how her Christmas holiday was. The driver said it was really good and asked the customer about her's. The homeowner explained that her husband had cancer, and he was very sick during the holiday season. The Fed Ex driver said she really did not know how to respond, so she changed the subject and told her customer to have a good day. Fed Ex drivers often experience chatting with the customers, which makes it difficult when they have over a hundred stops a day. However, this time was different. As the driver continued on her route, she could not get that one specific customer off of her mind. After twenty more stops, the driver felt like she had to go back. Even though she didn't have the time, she turned her truck around and headed back to her customer's home.

The driver hopped out of the truck and when the lady saw her coming up the driveway, she broke out into a big smile. The lady came out onto the porch, and the driver asked if she could pray with her. The driver prayed and afterwards, they hugged and both of them were crying.

Encouragers have to be flexible. You will not always get a notice before you are called on to encourage someone. It's good to be prepared. This skillset will just come with time, but being willing to share your time with others is key to being an encourager. It doesn't have to be a lot of time; in fact, it may only be a minute or two. However, it's impossible to be an encourager without investing some of your most precious commodity; your time.

As you become an encourager, you'll notice people will give you signs by the way they ask questions. For example, in the case of the homeowner and the delivery driver, notice how the lady asked the question. The Fed Ex driver did not necessarily want to know about her Christmas. Deep down, the homeowner wanted to prompt the driver to ask about her holiday because she needed someone to listen to her need. The driver was probably the first person she had seen that day.

Encouragers must have a keen awareness of a caregiver's need for a kind word. Frequently, the caregivers, whether medical staff or family members, need as much encouraging as the patient. The patient is usually not in control of the situation. He or she did not choose to be afflicted with a particular condition. However, the caregiver chooses to help. Oftentimes, especially when caregivers are family, they can feel hopeless about being able to comfort the patient, and they might need to vent their frustrations. It's important for caregivers to also have an encourager to listen. Active listening is an important skill for an encourager.

You might ask, *What is an active listener?* It's looking the person who is talking in their eyes the whole time they are speaking, even letting them pause, if need be, to think because they are talking with their heart. You need to listen with your heart, not your ears alone. Let the world stop around them and give your undivided attention. A good rule of thumb is to be the listener you would want them to be when you are speaking. Listening starts a relational connection, which adds credibility to your encouragement. It is vital to be genuine in your caring, and most people can instantly tell if you are faking it. If you are not genuine, you can't be an encourager. The good news is you can be genuine in seconds, an hour, or two weeks. The time isn't the determinant; it's the encourager's attitude that makes the difference.

Encouragers cannot be self-centered. We all think about our goals, our day's activities, and ourselves, which is perfectly normal. One habit I find that keeps me in check is to start my day asking myself a simple question: *Whom can I encourage today?* This immediately drives my subconscious focus from "me to thee." Effective encouragers often try to think out their comments, which is a great way to guard their conversations. When you focus on discussions that build others up rather than tear people down, you can see real results. Here's another example. My wife, Sue, called my friend's wife to wish her a happy birthday. While she was on the phone, I asked her to inquire about my friend's health because I knew he was battling cancer. He had been pretty sick and was in bed, so my wife asked if he was up to calling me so that I could talk with him. Later that evening, he called, and I could tell his voice was very weak. I did not want to wear him out with a long call, so I tried to speed up the conversation. I wanted to say over the phone how special he had been to me since our first meeting more than thirty years ago.

This was especially important to me because this man was instrumental in helping me become the man I am today. He had been an encouragement to me over the years, and I wanted him to know that. Then our conversation evolved into the description of an encourager. I sensed the more we talked about encouragers, the more the conversation was lifting him up. I could tell his voice was getting stronger. I really think as he reflected back on his life, he was able to share stories that encouraged him by knowing there were hundreds of people for whom he was able to make a difference in their lives. I also knew that I was one of those stories.

He is the man that I referred to in an earlier chapter who was leading the workshop in Charlotte, where the man planned to take his own life after leaving the workshop he was giving. If you thought you could have encouraged someone not to commit suicide, would you choose to be an encourager? Suppose it was your husband, son, daughter, mom, dad, or close friend. Would that change your answer? According to the American Foundation For Suicide Prevention, 47,176 people took their own lives in 2017.[12] Each one of them was someone's son, daughter, brother, or close friend. An encourager can make a life altering impact in a split second when the focus shifts from "me to thee." Let me challenge you to look for someone to encourage today. Try it today, and consider making it a daily life goal. Whom can I serve by encouraging them?

The phone call with my friend lasted two hours and forty minutes. He told me the one thing an encourager must be able to do is to encourage himself while encouraging others. He's found learning to laugh is the best way to do it. The Bible says, "A merry heart does good like medicine." That is a Biblical principal from Proverbs 17:22 long before mental health studies proved laughter is a key to good mental health.

The Mayo Clinic has done case studies to show how laugher affects the body. If you would like to read more on this subject, you can find it on their website. Permission was granted for us to print a few of them.

A sense of humor can't cure all ailments, but data is mounting about the positive things laughter can do.

Laughter has great short-term effects. When you start to laugh, it doesn't just lighten your load mentally; it induces physical changes in your body. Laughter can:

- **Stimulate many organs. Laughter enhances oxygen-rich air, stimulates your heart, lungs and muscles, and increases the endorphins that are released by your brain.**
- **Activate and relieve your stress response. A rollicking laugh fires up and then cools down your stress response, and it can increase and then decrease your heart rate and blood pressure.**
- **Soothe tension. Laughter can also stimulate circulation and aid muscle relaxation, both of which can help reduce some of the physical symptoms of stress.**
- *Improve your immune system. Negative thoughts manifest into chemical reactions that can affect your body by bringing more stress into your system and decreasing your immunity. By contrast, positive thoughts can actually release neuropeptides that help fight stress and, potentially, more serious illnesses.*
- *Relieve pain. Laughter may ease pain by causing the body to produce its own natural painkillers.*

Laughter makes it easier to cope with difficult situations. It helps you connect with other people. Many people experience depression, sometimes due to chronic illnesses. Laughter can help lessen your depression and anxiety and may make you feel happier.

Know what isn't funny. Don't laugh at the expense of others. Some forms of humor aren't appropriate. Discern a good joke from a bad or hurtful one.[13]

I was visiting with another friend, three-time NASCAR champion Cale Yarborough. I had two objectives for the meeting; check on him physically and get his advice on this book. I wanted to ask him if he had someone who had really encouraged him in his racing career. Before I got to ask the question, Cale said, "I lost a good friend this week: Glenn Woods."

Cale wanted to let Glenn's sons know how sorry he was to hear the news and how much their dad's friendship meant to him through the years. Glenn's relationship came at the turning point in Cale's career. Cale explained that Ford Motor Company believed they had put the partnership together with the Woods brothers, but Cale believed differently. At that time, this was one of the top teams in the NASCAR garage.

I believe God put Glenn and Cale together, and this relationship was a life changer for Cale's career and him personally. From the first day, Cale said, "I knew there was something different about the Woods brothers; they are top-notch Christian people."

When you dig into the experiences of successful people, you'll discover how encouragement has played a huge role in their lives. Cale also shared that he had different encouragers at different times in his life. Cale encourages me, especially as I look at a 36-acre pond that he dug by himself over six summers.

Cale said, "My neighbor told me I will never finish that pond." As he sat on the track hoe in the sweltering heat, he remembered what his neighbor had said, and the neighbor's discouragement rang in his head.

They are not going to be the winners; I will never give up, Cale thought. Encouragers make things happen. Discouragers watch things happen, and most everyone else wonders what happened.

vertical/For
Horizontal

This sign is one we want to relate to people everywhere when they see it. It's to remind them to be an encourager. To have maximum results we need vertical encouragement, to give horizontal encouragement.

Not about me

Encouragement is not about me or (you)

But the other person

It's about the.... Other person.

CHAPTER SIX

The Impact of
Discouragement

(Discouragers watch things happen)

WHEN I CONSIDERED the impact of discouragement, I wondered what society has lost because someone chose not to encourage another person. What if, at the very last moment just before a break-through medical discovery, the researcher was told he or she would never reach the goal? What if NASA scientists had told the Apollo astronauts they could never make it to the moon and return safely to the Earth?

What if, just before someone discovered the cure for cancer, he or she gave up because of the discouragement from the people around him or her? Maybe our world could have already had that next great invention. We must realize the synergistic power that is derived from working together to make things happen. Think about the giant California redwood trees. Some of those massive trees grow to be forty feet in diameter and three hundred feet tall. Did you know they only grow in groves where their underground roots intertwine and draw strength from each other? If those trees need each other to support their massive height, how much more do human beings need each other?

We need each other's support to accomplish great tasks as well. To discourage is to stunt development, desire, and growth. I was talking to a family member about this topic, and we agreed about the negative power of discouragement. "Let me tell you a story about my son when teachers told him he was a poor reader," she said. Her son accepted their opinion as gospel fact, and he did not read for a couple years.

Then, one day after changing schools, one of his new teachers wanted to move him into an accelerated reading group. My family member informed the teacher that the boy was not a good reader. The teacher disagreed strongly. "He is a good reader." She moved him to a new reading group, and he went on to become the top reader in the new group. Teachers have a great responsibility to encourage students to reach their greatest potential and to avoid discouraging students by harping on weaknesses.

Are you familiar with Les Brown's powerful story? At six weeks old, Les and his twin brother were given up for adoption to Mime Brown. Ms. Brown cleaned houses to support the family.

When Les went to school, he made it to the fourth grade, and the teachers declared him mentally uneducable. The story does not end there.

One day, Les was in a high school classroom, waiting for another student, when the teacher asked him to write something on the chalkboard. Les said, "I can't. I am not one of your students." The teacher said that did not matter and asked him to do it anyway. Les responded, "Sir, I can't. I am mentally retarded. I cannot write or spell."

The teacher came from behind his desk and told Les he didn't ever want to hear him say that again. "If you are hungry, you can do anything in life you want to do," said the teacher. Les took that to heart and never looked back. Les has served as an Ohio State House Representative and has been well paid to speak all over the world to as many as eighty thousand people.

These are two cases, but they represent countless examples of where teachers have made judgments about a student that were completely wrong. Teachers and other professionals have to walk a fine line based on their training, but in my opinion, whenever possible, they should err on the side of encouragement, not pronouncement of failure or impossibility. Only God knows our potential because He created us.

It's important to find ways to encourage people without intentionally leading them down a negative path. For example, it would not be appropriate to lead a five feet tall, fully grown man to believe he is going to play center position in the National Basketball Association. However, that person may be an all-star point guard. We must be careful not to bring damage to a person who could change history. We don't have a clue about whom that might be. Remember, Thomas Edison was told he was stupid by his schoolteachers.

Walt Disney was told by his teachers he did not have an imagination. These were schoolteachers, but anyone who teaches has a great responsibility to not discourage.

In Singapore, there is a place called Bird Corner. For thousands of years, every Sunday morning, local residents bring their birds in bamboo cages with very ornate porcelain or ivory feeding bowls. This place is for people to drink tea and socialize, but it is primarily for the old birds to teach the young birds a new song. The older birds teach the younger birds to sing stronger and sweeter. Amazingly, some of these birds will sing for fifteen years. It is important for the birds to be there every week, so if you can't make it, you send your bird with a friend.

When we discourage people by being inappropriately critical, we divide society. Discouragement can destroy friendships, families, churches, cities, and countries. I have a friend who gets very excited about every idea or involvement that he or his family members are engaging in, but if it is my idea, he wants to challenge it or not really listen to hear the details to see if it is a good idea or not. It is extremely difficult to build a strong relationship with someone who discouraging.

My friend, unfortunately, is a red light because all he does is tear me down. He may do many things well, but he destroys our relationship through discouragement. Most red lights do not think they are discouragers because they are blind to their own dysfunction. The only hope for change in them is for someone who truly cares about them to encourage them to consider the truth. Change is a voluntary behavior, but they must desire the change. If we encourage one another, we can teach each other a new song.

QUESTIONS TO CONSIDER

1. What is the most damaging thing a discouragement does?

2. Who is affected by discouragement?

3. Who is the only person who truly knows your potential?

4. How can discouragement change history?

5. Can you give an example of how discouragement changed history?

6. Do you believe that if citizens chose to encourage others, national healing could begin and be sustained?

7. Who is the best person to start a movement to be an encourager?

8. When should you start, if not now?

9. We all need an accountability partner to help remind us on our journey for change.

Who is that person for you?

CHAPTER SEVEN

The Power of a Wife's Encouragement

IN THIS CHAPTER, I will share a very personal perspective on the power of a wife's encouragement. During the introduction, I shared how Sue made a decision to encourage me during some very dark times in our marriage. If it sounds like I am repeating this, it is worth repeating if it can save one marriage. I want to share more details, so if you're a wife, a husband, single, divorced, or widowed, you can learn about encouragement in a marriage.

There is a long list of issues that can strain any relationship; however, I believe the one thing that will put more stress on any relationship is the lack or misuse of money to provide for your family. This is where our story begins. I had finished my schooling and started our prosthetic career. Sue and I were slowly starting to build assets. We had bought a little house, we owned a couple of used cars, and our plan was moving right along. As we started becoming more financially successful, we started buying investment rental properties. That was also going well.

Then I had the opportunity to start a new business with a couple of friends. This is where I made a mistake. Even though Sue did not feel launching a new company was a good idea, I didn't listen, and I did it anyway. After four years, the economy crashed, and we had to consider closing the business; however, I really didn't want to shut it down.

We sold our investment properties to reduce overhead and just tried to hang on. After doing everything I knew to do, I felt there was no choice but to close the business. At that time, I still owed $90,000 at 19.5 percent interest. I contacted everyone we owed money to let them know I would pay them, but I needed a little time to make it happen.

Looking back on my experience, it was crystal clear how powerful Sue's encouragement was to me in our marriage. Here's why. Two years into the new business, the pressure had built up to the boiling point. I was only sleeping two to three hours per night.

Here's the key point. There was not a time during this experience that Sue ever blamed me for making an unwise decision to start the new business. She absolutely refused to even let it get into our conversation because she knew how it would impact me. She knew that I was taking responsibility for my actions and my family, and she did not need to beat me over the head even though she may have wanted to tell me a time or two.

There is a time and place for a strong rebuke. Had I been drinking my own "Kool-Aid" and living in denial, then we would have been in a different situation. If you are not owning up to the reality of your circumstances, then tough love may be the right answer, but this is not what we are talking about here. Just think about all the times when stuff happens, and everyone is operating in good faith. I didn't know the market would crash. I was doing my level best, but it just wasn't good enough. Sue could have beaten me up, and she would have technically been correct that it was my fault. I already knew it and owned it.

An encourager responds in this way rather than being opposed to speaking unkind words because it would not have helped our situation. More than likely, it could have ignited a fuse that would have burned up what was a good marriage. We all find ourselves in circumstances we don't like. However, in a case like this where a husband has done the absolute best he can, I would caution wives to avoid trying to forecast the future. Even though you may be extremely frustrated, make the choice to build up your husband.

I might suggest you also find a quiet time to tell your husband how you feel and why you have decided to encourage him. You love him, and you want him and your family to succeed. Too often, when a wife vents her feelings without careful consideration, it can absolutely destroy her husband. This can lead to even more horrific and predictable results. A wife can destroy a husband's confidence in himself because he wants to impress her more than anyone on the planet. Sadly, many marriages end because the wife continues to beat her husband up and inadvertently encourages him to find encouragement elsewhere. Please don't think I'm excusing adultery; I am just saying you are creating the environment for disaster in your marriage. I'm simply pointing out the painful consequences that can result when discouragement rules the roost. What if my wife had not made the choice to build me up and encourage me to succeed once again? Ultimately, with God's leading, we worked through this painful period in our lives, and we were able to pay off every penny of the $90,000 debt obligation.

As we came out on the other side of the financial meltdown, we built up a successful business that made it possible to purchase four airplanes, a condo at the beach, our son's college education, and two new homes and have a debt-free retirement. The greatest lessons and rewards were learning to trust God during the most hopeless times in our life together.

The reason I share our success is not to impress you with material blessing, but rather to impress upon you how Sue's encouragement changed the course of our lives.

Perhaps you or someone you know is at a similarly crucial point in their lives. Consider encouraging them to study the power of an encouraging wife. Encouragement always gives a fantastic rate of return. The manifestation may not be in material wealth. You may have already been through a failed marriage and hope to learn lessons that will help in your second marriage. My position here is not to judge but to encourage you to own the responsibility to encourage your spouse and be honest about the situation.

Living a life without regrets is a worthy goal. Encouragement is a powerful tool to reach that long-term milestone. When we practice this skill at home, we can also transfer it to our kids, at work, in church, and across our nation.

QUESTIONS TO CONSIDER

1. What is one of the first things a wife must do when her husband makes a bad financial decision?
    •   What are the potential outcomes if a wife chooses discouragement?
    •   What are the possibilities if a wife chooses to encourage her husband?

The answers to these questions for Sue and I are very easy when looking into the rearview mirror of life. You may be in the midst of a storm, and I hope you will give great consideration to learning from this simple principle of encouragement (building up not destroying). Please learn from our experience, and take the road less traveled.

CHAPTER EIGHT

Husband, Empower Your Soulmate

As I shared in the previous chapter, what follows is from personal experience in our marriage. The lessons below are not theoretical, but they come from the school of "hard knocks" that we attended for more years than I wanted. Hopefully, you will be a quick study and be able to apply or share these lessons where appropriate. Here's the good news: your marriage will work if you and your spouse are willing to work at it. I am a firm believer in the fact that when two people in a marriage respect each other's role, the synergy that develops is powerful. When a husband embraces and empowers the strength of his wife, the result is an empowered soulmate. When a husband and wife enjoy a oneness relationship, they can change the world, and as you probably guessed, encouragement is the bedrock of such a powerful marriage.

One of the fastest ways for husbands to destroy an opportunity to empower their brides is to not include them in any decision making. Many times, husbands make the mistake of thinking that a lot of our decisions are not important decisions, so they don't bother to ask for their wife's input. Here's the problem: what a husband thinks is a big decision and what a wife thinks is a big decision can be miles apart. Husbands make assumptions that unknowingly create massive stress in the relationship. There is an easy fix for this problem. Err on the side of conservative decision making.

Husbands should discuss mostly everything with their wives. Obviously, you can take that to the ridiculous extreme. It's much easier to come to agreement on places for independent decision making, like financial spending limits or household decisions. When a husband has respect for his wife, he wants her counsel, and it adds strength to the decision. When practiced over time, husbands come to recognize the unique gift wives have at seeing what we husbands may not be able to see. At the same time, when a husband respects his wife enough to ask for her opinion, the wife may be wise enough to defer to other experts when necessary. For example, unless the wife is an attorney, she will likely recommend seeking legal counsel when it is important. The point is that nobody else has the relational bond of a wife to a husband in a marriage, so it is only common sense that this must be the priority relationship. I do not make any major decisions anymore without running it by my wife, and if I'm not sure if it's a major decision, you guessed it. I chat with Sue. Most of the time, she goes along with my recommendation, especially now that we have a much better track record.

Over time, as I have empowered her as my soulmate, her support as my number one encourager grows and gets stronger over time. One day on the way home from church recently, I had an epiphany. Sue and I were talking about encouragers as we pulled into the garage, and a thought hit me that I had never really expressed to her. I looked into her eyes and said, "Honey, everything we have is not about Bob; it's about you. I have thought about this a lot. If you had not encouraged me during our darkest hours, I can assure you, we would not be here." Sue responded quietly, "Well, I don't know about that." I insisted that she not argue with me because I am not even sure that I would not have committed suicide were it not for her encouragement. I was in such a painful, dark place. I was so tired from not sleeping for four years that I could not think straight about anything. During this very challenging time I learned something very important to me: as long as I have breath and a heartbeat, there is hope. Don't give up! If you don't remember anything else in this book, especially if you are struggling or you know someone who is in a dark place, please cry out to God for help and, again, remember: as long as you have breath and a heartbeat, there is still hope.

QUESTIONS TO CONSIDER

1. What is the first thing husbands should always remember when making major decisions?

2. What is the next step for the husband when he did not consult his wife before making a major decision, if he wants to keep her on the team?

3. What did I say was the most important thing I learned that made a major difference in my relationship with my wife that you can never forget?

CHAPTER NINE

Encouragement Goes Viral

WILLIAM MCRAVEN, A retired United States Navy Admiral and former SEAL who served as the commander of the United States Special Operations Command, addressed his alma mater with a powerful commencement message.[14] If you continue the viral influence factor through one more generation, you could affect more than the entire population of the United States and a good chunk of the civilized world. This is very encouraging to know that it is possible to have a major impact on our country with this timely and powerful message.

As I travel and share my assessment of our country's condition with fellow citizens, I find very little disagreement. In order to influence millions of Americans to change, the first step is to get a small group (like the four thousand people Admiral McRaven suggested) to understand why being an encourager is good for them. Once a person understands the value for himself and commits to working on making his own life better, he establishes the foundation for viral growth.

As people start to share their stories on social media, this will start the process that can cause this project to go viral. Imagine the first person in our network who tells his encouragement story, how he found hope and then decided not to take his life. Think about what will happen when a scientist explains he or she did not give up on finding a cure for a dreaded disease because someone encouraged him or her to press on. Americans will find hope again by the very action of encouraging others.

When a person encourages someone, they receive as much, sometimes more, back than was ever given to the person being encouraged. It will help accelerate this encouraging vision for our country and the world when each one gets another person involved. People, not projects, are what really matter. More than anything else, we must realize the people placed in our paths need encouraging. The tide will start to turn when an army of people who are solely focused on this agenda understand the power of a win-win program to serve others through encouragement.

The encourager becomes encouraged, and the experience of encouraging helps accomplish the goal.

In our present social climate, most people live in an environment where they are very skeptical of everyone. Let me remind you, most people tend to forget what they hear but rarely forget what they see. They are searching for genuine people they can trust and share their concerns with. As relationships blossom and people meet dependable, quality people with whom they develop trust, then influence grows. As we each encourage those with whom we share a trusted relationship, the next generation of encouragers will get in gear, naturally. Encouragement gives hope to the hopeless.

Let's cut to the chase. I want to change the way most Americans think, which has led us down a primrose path to a hopeless, divided society. We are so divided racially. I once had a black lady from Jamaica ask me if I knew the black crab and grey crab story. I told her that I wasn't familiar with it. She said to me, "Black people in Jamaica know this story, and you need to hear it."

Imagine two buckets of crabs, one bucket of grey crabs and the other with black crabs. In each bucket, you put one black crab and one grey crab. If you leave them alone for a few minutes, both crabs will find their way out. Next, put ten black crabs in one bucket and ten grey crabs in the other bucket and leave them overnight. When you come back in the morning, you'll find all ten black crabs will still be in the bucket.

When you check the other bucket, you will be surprised to find all of the grey crabs are gone. What's the difference? If you had a hidden camera watching the black crabs, you'd see, as soon as one starts to climb the bucket wall, the other crabs pull him down. This never stops, so they are stuck in their hopelessness. This is where America is today. The grey crabs do things differently. You may ask, "How so?" As the first grey crab moves up the wall, his closest buddy hooks to his claw and pushes him up the wall and out of the bucket. The next grey crab repeats the process until they have pulled the last of the ten crabs over the wall and out of the bucket.

What can we learn from grey crabs? If we cannot learn to work together, we will never get out of the crisis this country is in, and this will destroy America. Our ancestors sailed the tiny Mayflower across the dangerous ocean nearly four hundred years ago to seek a different way of life than what America is today. They chose to leave tyranny and follow God's calling.

We face a similar choice. Candidly, it does not matter who gets credit for starting this movement to change the course of America. We have to get started before it is too late. It's about getting started, committing, and seeing it through. Knowing about the problem in this country is nothing; doing something about the problem is everything.

To initiate and follow through on this massive project will take commitment from millions of people who engage and help raise the required budget to get the message out. What is it worth to save our country? If you consider American spending, the National Retail Federation reports that in 2017, $9.1 billion was spent on Halloween, and $9 billion was spent on costumes and candy last Halloween. It sure seems like this project should be something that Americans would participate in to help support so many and serve so many more. I don't mind asking for help to save this nation, especially when I think about how many Americans through history have given up everything, including their lives.

When we commit to live a life of encouragement, we ensure our service members did not die in vain. This message must go viral, but the good news is that we already know it can. Think of all the videos and photos you've seen on social media with heartwarming, encouraging stories of neighbors helping neighbors. What we are really talking about here is simply organizing and encouraging more of the same, especially once people understand the exponential impact their actions have on others.

I believe if America is to survive as founded, we do not have a choice. There are countless organizations that hate the foundational construction of America, and they spend millions of dollars every day to promote division. Their primary agenda and goals are to destroy this country internally, and sadly, it is working.

A few years ago, when I started investing considerable personal time and resources to explore how to rebuild America, I often heard, "Somebody needs to do something." I'm inviting you to join me on a journey of hope and inspiration, one that can be started without a single penny, but rather with a kind word. Together, we can start a viral trend of encouragement that we know produces powerful results. As the movement grows, it will attract more resources and organizations that will help us get the word out at scale. When it does, we will reach millions at home and abroad.

Please remember, this is not a political agenda, although people will demand politicians must do their part ethically, morally, and financially, on both sides of the aisle.

Pastors and priests across all denominations, serving every race, must carry this biblical message forward.

Americans will win when those with strong platforms of influence put away their personal pride to help deliver this message. Then, and only then, can we halt the catastrophic impact that will destroy the USA.

QUESTIONS TO CONSIDER

1.   Will you be an encourager?

2.   Will you help encouragement go viral by encouraging others?

3.   Will you set daily, weekly, monthly, and yearly goals for yourself?

4.   What can you learn from the black crab illustration?

5.   What can you learn from the grey crab illustration?

6.   When you privately look in the mirror, which crab do you most closely associate with and why?
     1.   Grey crabs (lift up)
     2.   Black crabs (tear down)

CHAPTER TEN

Don't Give Up

WHEN I HEAR this phrase, my mind immediately goes to Sir Winston Churchill, Great Britain's Prime Minister during World War II, its darkest hour. Churchill was faced with one of the toughest decisions in all of history. Great Britain was nearing a conflict with Germany, and Churchill reached out for help from every country in the free world, but no country came to its assistance. At that point, all Churchill could do was encourage his countrymen to never surrender. On June 4, 1940, at the end of his address to the House of Commons, Sir Winston Churchill shared these most famous words: [15]Even though large tracts of Europe and many old and famous States have fallen or may fall into the grip of the Gestapo and all the odious apparatus of Nazi rule, we shall not flag or fail. We shall go on to the end, we shall fight in France, we shall fight on the seas and oceans, we shall fight with growing confidence and growing strength in the air, we shall defend our Island, whatever the cost may be, we shall fight on the beaches, we shall fight on the landing grounds, we shall fight in the fields and in the streets, we shall fight in the hills; we shall never surrender, and even if, which I do not for a moment believe, this Island or a large part of it were subjugated and starving, then our Empire beyond the seas, armed and guarded by the British Fleet, would carry on the struggle, until, in God's good time, the New World, with all its power and might, steps forth to the rescue and the liberation of the old. This is a real-world example of *The Power of an Encourager*™. The Prime Minister's unrelenting and passionate encouragement to British subjects and to those who would ultimately become his allies against the Axis Powers helped usher in the support necessary to win the greatest fight on Earth.

I commissioned the design of a lapel pen that says, "Be an Encourager." Frequently, I'm asked about the pin. This gives me an opening to challenge people to join us as some of our first encouragers. What follows are a few of the points I make during these impromptu conversations. I've already shared my favorite one-liner with you: "No matter how dark life may look, as long as you have breath and a heartbeat, there is hope." As you get more knowledgeable from reading this book and using the "Encouragers Daily Planner," you'll develop a sense of the need to encourage as well as how to effectively engage.

One of the most common missing elements for citizens in our society is a trustworthy person they can talk with face-to-face. It may seem odd, but take note how often couples or families are continuously scrolling through their phones at a public restaurant.

The people never talk to each other. With the growing suicide rate, people need a sounding board, frequently, with someone who is a good listener. My son in Hong Kong recently shared a story about a family where the dad moved to a larger city from a small town to find work.

The mother could not deal with the move, so she abandoned her husband and their four small children. With a busy father and a missing mother, the children lost hope and all four committed suicide. Can you imagine? Sadly, this happens in this country as well. The largest segment of suicide increase in our society is with ages 10–27 year old white males.

According to recent statistics from an AFSP report, we spent $69 billion in 2015 on those attempted suicides or self-inflicted injuries in America. According to Dr. Joshua Gordon, director of the National Institute of Mental Health (NIMH), America is the only country in the world where suicides are increasing, and we don't even know why.

Dr. Gordon went on to say the suicide rate in mostly all other countries is decreasing.[16]

I believe a divided spirit has invaded every sector of our country. This division has hatred attached to everything it touches. A suicide attempt is a clear indication that something is gravely wrong in a person's life. No matter the race or age of the person, or how rich or poor they are, it is true that most people who die by suicide have a mental or emotional disorder. The most common underlying disorder is depression. Thirty to seventy percent of suicide victims suffer from major depression or bipolar (manic-depressive) disorder. In addition, many suicides are committed by people who have known mental health issues.[17]

Hopelessness is a driving force in mental health decline. Most people living in despair don't know what to do. Encouragers can help support these people as they work through challenging times simply by spending time listening to their concerns. This is especially true with older men and women. There are different times during the year that can be especially difficult for senior citizens, especially if they have lost their spouse and live without family close by. Sending a card or joining them for a special event will encourage them to know someone cares about them. Even a short phone call to start the new year off will give a senior hope. Remember, it's often the smallest gesture that can be a *big* encouragement.

You don't have to be an excellent communicator to encourage someone. I recently observed a young, mentally handicapped lady encourage a man who was dying from cancer. After her visit, the man told me, "That young lady will never know how meaningful that visit was for me." She likely never knew the powerful impact she had on him. **Little things can make a big difference**.

On the other side of the coin, an encourager must learn to guard his or her tongue. First of all, I recommend you never speak about others when they are not present, unless you have their permission to share an experience. There are certainly times when you can share an anecdote or incident that can be traced back to a particular person if that story can't help another. Avoid anything that may be perceived as gossip. Careless speech can hurt deeply. Little things can also do the biggest damage. Always remember, when you speak about someone, you are either building him or her up or tearing him or her down. It's never right to make judgment statements about someone who may not respond the way you feel he or she should. I call this "character assassination." I hear this quite often from every category I can think of. I have started stopping in the middle of a sentence, even to my wife, if I border on character assassination. It will destroy relationships and create division.

For instance, have you ever had a person ask you what you think about someone else just so that person can tell you what he or she thinks? This almost always leads to character assassination or gossip. As an encourager, you must shut this down. This destroys trust, and you can encourage the would-be-gossiper to change his or her ways. Many times, when people don't respond the way we want them to, we may be tempted to throw them under the bus, so to speak.

Here's another true story to illustrate my point. A friend of mine had a guy with a drug problem come by his office and ask for help. The kind of help the guy requested was not what you would have expected. He didn't ask for money. He wanted help getting his life straightened out.

I received another call from my friend updating me on the guy with the drug problem. The pastor suggested that he enroll in a church program to help him and another program to secure housing. The guy agreed to enroll but only stayed for two days. My friend's excitement left when the guy disappeared, but he never gave up on trying to locate him. Weeks later, the guy came back to his office with a story that everything had been stolen, and he was unable to contact him while he was in another city. Since the guy only had the clothes on his back and an extreme case of hunger, my friend fed him and put him up for one night.

The next morning, my friend took him to a shelter. This is an encourager in action. I am so proud of my friend and his persistence to never give up, even when the guy he was working with made another bad decision.

"You cannot beat a person who will not quit."

—*Babe Ruth*[18]

QUESTIONS TO CONSIDER

1. Who will you call to begin encouraging?

2. Which senior citizens would be encouraged by hearing from you after the holidays and throughout the year?

3. Why is it so bad to give your opinion of someone behind his or her back?

4. Is there anyone you have given up on that you can reconnect with and encourage?

5. Where do most people go when things are looking hopeless?

70

CHAPTER ELEVEN

The Power of Relationships

IN CHAPTER FOUR, I introduced you to Muhtar Kent, Chairman of the board of directors of the Coca-Cola Company, who says he never eats a meal alone because he is passionate about taking every opportunity to build relationships. I agree for many reasons. First, this gives you an opportunity not only to encourage others, but to also be encouraged with fellowship at the dining table. Contrast this with sitting alone, perhaps in a depressed mood, listening to people at the next table having a great time. Which would you prefer?

Mr. Kent's next point is that meals are a perfect time to start a relationship with someone or develop an already existing relationship. Muhtar Kent is one of the busiest men in the world, which means he has to maximize his time to its fullest. There is no excuse for anyone who says he or she is too busy to have relationships. The real issue is that relationships take effort. A lot of people are just plain lazy and self-centered. Investing in others begins with a keen desire to serve others. Encouragers know how, or they are willing to learn how, to build relationships, which will broaden their influence across the spectrum. Regardless of your experience, if you want to make a difference in this world, continually developing your relationship-building skills is crucial. In my view, there are two different types of relationships to develop. One is the vertical relationship we touched on earlier with a higher power. From my Christian worldview, this higher power is the creator of the universe, the triune God, which is the Father, His Son Jesus Christ and the Holy Spirit. If you'd like to know more about the ultimate encourager, Jesus Christ, I recommend a good King James Bible, start in proverbs or New King James Study Bible. (Charles Stanley) One of the benefits of developing a vertical relationship with God is that it's much harder to see yourself as the center of the universe. When our ego is in check, it's easier to encourage others because we realize we all have issues. As a Christian, I know I'm a sinner, and God is no respecter of persons.

In other words, whether I'm worth a billion dollars or twelve cents, in the eyes of the Lord, I'm worth no more than you are. God invites every person to discover His plan for eternity.

This vertical relationship also supercharges the power we possess internally to share hope with those who need encouragement. I mentioned earlier in the book that I read a chapter of Proverbs every day. This is part of what I call the three P's: purpose, passion, and preparation. Finding your purpose will do so much to help you understand your self-worth, especially when you understand God put you on this earth at this time for a very specific purpose.

When you are encouraged, your focus changes because a passion will develop within you to become an encourager. We must prepare ourselves to carefully consider relationships and not allow our passion to override discernment. Relationships are a two-way street, which means you must be willing to decide the level of investment you will make in another person. It's also important to look at the long haul, not just a brief stint. As you look at what you can give to another person, you also have to think about what you expect from the other person. Is it an appropriate balance? If you don't take the time to think about the relationship details, you may be pursuing a relationship that will fail. If you are too zealous, you may end up being a doormat if the other person is only looking to benefit himself or herself and not you. This would lead to a red light relationship. Strong relationships built around encouragement require preparation. In some cases, just a quick thought on the ideal place to meet or best time of the day may create a scenario that optimizes your time together and allows you the room to build trust.

As you prepare and communicate with the other person, you'll find a good relationship is balanced and fruitful. You will be an encourager to them, and usually, your time together will encourage you. Guard a relationship like this carefully because they don't come around every day. When you have a balanced, encouraging relationship, your life will seem so much brighter. Your energy level will be up. It will be harder to have a bad day, and you will feel like the birds sing better, the air is cleaner, and all is right with the world. The blessing of starting an honest, transparent relationship and keeping it that way is that it will get stronger over time, maybe perhaps for a lifetime. Obviously, in these few short pages, we can't get into all the dynamics of a strong relationship. We've been primarily referring to platonic, encouraging relationships, not necessarily marital ones.

However, it's important to note that from a biblical point of view, most of us are made with a void to be filled with a spouse. Adam had a void, and God filled it with his helpmate, Eve. I believe, for the most part, God wants you to get that need filled too. There is a person somewhere to fill your void, and if you are still waiting for Mr. or Mrs. Right, my only caution is not to get in a hurry. Your skill at building encouraging relationships will likely prepare you for the time when the right person comes along; just be patient. Getting the wrong person is worse than being single. A strong marriage will bring joy to your life and will be a powerful encouragement to others. To have friends, we must be friendly. Become the best possible friend you can be, and others will be attracted to you. That is relationship empowerment.

Every part of life is built on relationships: who you marry, where you work, who you socialize with, where you go to church. It's all about Relationships!

QUESTIONS TO CONSIDER

1. What does Muhtar Kent never do alone? Why?

2. What are the three P's that drive strong relationships?

3. Why is it important to have discernment in platonic and romantic relationships?

4. What are the top priorities in relationships you want to pursue? Why?

CHAPTER TWELVE

Personal Stories of Encouraging People

WHILE WRITING THIS *book, many folks wanted to share their stories with me. I thought it would be interesting for you to hear some of the stories. The impact that encouragement has had on people is incredible.*

Let me start by telling you a little bit about a lady I was introduced to by a longtime friend. After meeting her and finding out that she is from Uganda, I introduced the concept of the book that I was writing to her to encourage Americans. She immediately said to me that this book is not just a book for America; it is for the world. As time and things have evolved, I agree. Our friendship developed, and she asked me to meet with the mayor of a small town in South Carolina: Lake City. I proceeded to set up the appointment, and she agreed to go with me. I had never met this man. My intent was to share with him about the Winning America project and tell him about this new book that I am writing on encouragement. As we walked to his office, he said he was dealing with an issue that he was not sure how to handle. We left it at that and proceeded to give him the overview of the project and the book. As we were getting ready to leave, he said, "Now that we have talked, I believe I have the answer of how to deal with the issue at hand. Would you let me tell you my story?"

Lovith Anderson's Story

Lovith Anderson said he was introduced to alcohol at the age of thirteen. Peer pressure led him to his first drink. By the time he entered college, he was an alcoholic. His drinking was so bad that it was impossible to keep his grades up, so he flunked out. Then a drunk driving conviction caused him to wake up for a little while. Lovith decided to move from Lake City to Pasadena, California, to be with family members. It really seemed to be the right decision. He was able to find a job and a woman he wanted to spend the rest of his life with. They married and was blessed with two boys. Within a year and a half, he had gotten on drugs that led to him losing his job and family. Life was hopeless.

He decided to end it all. It was Super Bowl Sunday 1987. His plan was to be on the front page of the paper. He went to a spot in Pasadena that had the nickname "Suicide Bridge." There he would end it all. Lovith climbed up on the bridge, preparing to take the leap. He felt as if he had let so many people down. He said he had failed everyone. Just before he jumped, a car came and stopped, and someone yelled, "Don't do it!" Lovith felt like this was a message from God giving him a second chance. He then went through drug therapy and returned to Lake City where he is making a huge impact on his city. He has started so many rehab programs to keep others from falling into the same traps he did as a 13-year-old boy. Lovith is proud of Lake City and its history, from its agricultural roots to having one of its native sons go into space (Ronald E. McNair) and a native daughter being recognized as one of the smartest businesswomen in the world (Darla Moore), Anderson said.

"Never Give Up."

—*Mayor of Lake City, SC,*
Lovith Anderson.

My Wife Sue's Story

As I was walking into the auditorium for a Sunday morning church service, I happened to meet one of our elderly widow ladies who had just lost her husband a few months earlier. I put my arm around her, hugged her, and asked how she was doing. We exchanged small talk, and I went on my way to the choir. That morning during the service, my sister, who was also in the choir, noticed that this lady was crying. Thinking she was still grieving over her husband, on Monday my sister went and bought a bouquet of flowers to take to her. When she arrived at the lady's home and mentioned that she had seen her crying during the service, the widow explained how I had given her a hug and spoken to her so sweetly. It really touched her heart and made her feel so good.

*"It's the little things that can make
the biggest difference."*

—Sue Skelton

This next story *is written by a long-time friend and maybe needs
a little explanation because it is quite long. Robert Griffith is a friend
from West Virginia, but I did not know him in West Virginia. It was
not until he moved to Winston Salem, NC, where he joined a gospel
music group that I was associated with that I got to know him. Robert
is a very talented musician and songwriter. He really can do anything
he sets his mind to. I am trying to set this up as to say we know people,
but do we really know them? Do we ever spend the time to get to know
their heart? A relationship is not with the head, but the heart. You can
better encourage someone when you can read their heart and experience their joy or their sadness. After I read Robert's story, I realized I
only knew the musician and the songwriter. That wasn't Robert at all.*

Robert Griffith's Story

I wasn't quite four, when I remember encountering my first
"encourager." I'm not sure Uncle Rome knew that's what he was
doing, and it may have only happened once in my life, but, in my
little three-year-old mind, it occurred every time he and Aunt
Pearl made that 5-mile journey to our little house in the country.
Ultimately, at some time during the visit, Uncle Rome would sit
down on the front porch swing, and I'd climb up beside him. As
we'd begin to swing, I'd lay my head over on his lap, and he'd
rub his hand across my buzz-cut hair, pat me on top of the head,
and say, "There's a lot going on in that little head." Throughout

my life, I have been careful to be gentle and deliberate when speaking to children and adults, alike. I purpose to highlight a positive, affirming, and truthful attribute I see in them, knowing that my statement to them may become an unforgettable source of strength they'll remember for years to come.

Eventually, I became Uncle Rome. Why? The answer is curious. For years, I thought it was simply because I wanted to be to others what he had been to me: an unforgettable encouragement. That was certainly a part of it then, and now too, for the most part. But several years ago, my family observed my "above and beyond" behavior toward others and asked, "Why do you go overboard in what you do for people?" My answer was: "Love, of course! Because," I'd say, "love suffers long and is kind, doesn't build itself up, thinks no evil, but rejoices in the truth. It bears all things, believes all things, hopes all things, endures all things. You know, 1 Corinthians 13: love never fails, right?" They said, "Well, that sounds pretty good and very religious, but you'd never go overboard like that for us!" Wow, now there was a wake up call that was impossible to dismiss. It was an observation I would ponder for years to come.

Eventually, that "love" nearly caused me to kill myself. What I discovered was I was going overboard for others because I was looking for that same type of affirmation from others. I had such a poor self-image and couldn't believe anyone could just love me for being myself. So I went out of my way for them, hoping to earn a place of friendship with them. There came a time when all of the "selfless" love I had invested in a ministry relationship with a few individuals was met with a violation of trust and betrayal. I was devastated and became suicidal.

I was never good enough, handsome enough, strong enough, tall enough, rich enough, talented enough, or thoughtful enough. And it was always easy to find family members or associates steeped in religion who were happy to fan the flames of those guilt-laden, self-imposed inadequacies. Yet, I never lacked attention growing up. My family performed Christian music on stages around the country from the time I was five years old. In 1969, when I was twelve, and for the two years following, I played dinner music on the Hammond organ at a local restaurant at South Charleston, West Virginia. In my high school days, we did gospel music once a week on a popular, live country music television show that aired daily on Channel 8, Charleston, for years. When I was seventeen, I left West Virginia and moved to North Carolina to spend the following thirty-five years making a living writing, singing, arranging, publishing, and performing gospel music all over the world.

There was no lack of attention. The problem was, I totally associated my perception of who I was with what I did. It was easy to feel loved and appreciated when I was at the organ, producing behind the television camera, or being in front of the camera performing or on a stage. But when I was out from under the lights, I was a guilty sinner, unworthy of the love, admiration, or affection of anybody because I was not using my gift. I knew the drill. We all knew the parable of the ten talents from the New Testament. After all, it had come from the pulpit and been pounded into my head for years and went something like this: "When God gives you a gift, you have to use it, or He'll take it away from you and give it to someone else." To most, including me, that translated into commerce. I always had to be preparing, promoting, or performing my "gift" as a vocation and making a living from it to be approved of God! Sound familiar?

Growing up in the western Christian environment, I was introduced to Guilt early on. The well-meaning preacher man made our initial introductions. Guilt and I became fast friends when we were just children. Mama, along with most religious folks in those days, felt like my new friend, Guilt, would help me walk the straight and narrow way. My childhood mentor soon became a mistress of delusion. She robbed me of my innocence, and I never went to bed without her, at least until I was in my early sixties. At the time of this writing, it's been over ten years since I retired from a musical life on the road. Only in the last year has a statement a trusted, missionary friend made to me early in 1978 started to make sense. I had been lamenting to her concerning my position, my disposition, or whatever unreasonable expectation I had placed upon my God and myself. I was seeking some word of wisdom from her. She listened with a compassionate ear and wasted no time in giving me some of the most profound advice of my lifetime. It was summed up in one sentence. "Robert," she said, "don't ever underestimate your influence." Everyone has a sphere of influence. You may not believe yourself to be "influential" from a societal perspective, and yet you are. If you go out and integrate with the public at all, someone is watching. "Oh," you say, "I only go out to the grocery store or to church or synagogue once a week."

Then, my friend, you have a sphere of influence. Is it your belief that you have nothing to offer? Do you think you lack the talent, skill, or personality that seems to come naturally to others to interact with folks? Well, perhaps it isn't as natural for you, but let me ask you this: when your church family or grocery store attendant sees you coming, do you suppose they're murmuring softly under their breath, "Oh my heavens, here comes that sourpuss again," or "Oh, here comes the one who always greets me with a smile and a kind word, and I know I'll feel better after having interacted with them today"? You do have an influence. Most people I meet on a daily basis now have no idea who I was. I have nothing staged to give them no piano, no songs, no lights, no cameras. Everyone I meet isn't going to be like me when I was a kid. They'll not be in a position to lay their head in my lap and receive affirmation from me like I got from Uncle Rome. You know, Uncle Rome didn't get anything out of that: no money, no accolades, no rewards or recognition here on earth. What he got out of it was the blessing of planting a seed of encouragement that, incidentally, he never was able to watch take root and grow. He died of cancer many years before the seed he planted sprang up and became any kind of recognizable plant.

Yet, he is a part of every success I've ever known. He didn't sing. He didn't play. My success became his significance. Perhaps this is the way one can really live forever. I tell the story of Uncle Rome here, fifty-eight years after it happened. You read it and remember the Uncle Rome in your life. You share the story with others, and Uncle Rome lives on. Now, I listen to a spirit of love as I make eye contact with those I encounter. I've had many years to learn to discern what to say, if anything other than a smile and a nod. When it's time to speak or to do the work of encouragement, the wonderful truth is, I may never know who it is that word is to or what it may mean to them. I do know, according to 1 Corinthians chapter 13, that "love never fails." If something never fails, that means that something only succeeds. So, I have the blessing of success in love. Life is my stage, my instrument, my camera, my audience. It's yours too. Be an encourager, expecting nothing. Each time you do, you'll receive the bountiful reward of significance, being only where you can be, saying only what you can say to the audience of one you have been placed in front of because of the unique child of the Most High you are. 1 John 3:2: "Beloved, now are we the sons of God..." Right now. Walk in the light of your Father, and let that light of encouragement shine through you.

—Robert Griffith

My Son and Daughter-in-Law's Story:

Hi Grant & Rebecca,

This is Tom the "old man" at Plantation Baptist Church, where your son Harrison made an everlasting impression on me that will go with me through time and into eternity when I think of the expression he made—"But I don't want him to leave"—and he hugged me. I can't express how I felt at that moment. The thought of the incident helps me through bad days. Hallelujah!!!!!!!!! I hope you get this letter soon. I want to send you a Christmas gift. So let me know right away if you get this letter.

God bless you all, Tom

Hi Harrison!

Harrison is my grandson, who is nine years old during the writing of this book. You can be an encourager at any age!

"It's the little people who can make the biggest difference."

Teach your children to be encouragers at an early age. Still model it in front of them to be an encourager, and build up people, not tear them down.

When we come to the last story, each one has had a different flair. I trust you have been moved and challenged by each one. This story will tell you how many of Americans have grown up and how many still live like this today. This is also why I say 8 out of 10 people you meet on any given day are hurting. I believe we should want to make a difference in those people to make life a little more pleasant. Let's hope this is the only hell they ever experience. Join me in this rescue effort.

Hello Mr. Bob,

Tonight I couldn't sleep, as most nights lately, but tonight I was compelled to share my story with you. On tonight I'm feeling more down than usual, and I really need prayer and encouragement. When people hear my story, they oftentimes think I'm much older than what I am because I have experienced far greater than the average 34-year-old. I hope not to be too long-winded, and I may leave some parts out just because I feel it is no longer a part of my

story. Lastly, I may have quite a few grammatical
errors because I just don't feel like going back to
fix them at 1:36 a.m. lol.

I have learned so much in the short time that I have met
you, which has caused me to think and evaluate parts of my life.
The other day you said, "The two most important events in
your life are the day you are born and the day you find out why."
Purpose...I have been searching for that for so long. I don't just
want to be here, but I want to make a difference while I'm here.
Mr. Bob, have you ever felt so tired, but yet you still wanted
to fulfill what God has for you to do, but you didn't know if
you could? I am mentally, spiritually, and physically tired. God
has given me a lot of gifts, and I thank him for them, but I am
still confused about my purpose. In my childhood, I told you I
grew up in a Christian home, but what I didn't tell you, despite
growing up in that type of environment, I had to learn who God
was for myself. I had lost my faith at around 12 years old because
my "Christian home" wasn't so Christian. My father, who was
a minister, would abuse my mother every day until the point
she ended up in ICU. I remember, as a little girl, watching my
father, who was supposed to be my protector, throw my mother
down the steps, punch her in the face, etc. I was the youngest
then, and I would watch one of my older sisters try to help, and
he would hit her. On some of his worst nights, he would take
an extension cord and wait until I got out of the tub and beat
me until I bled. He was on the police force as well, so when my
mother would call the police, he would sweet-talk them into
leaving. Back then I hated my father. I have always hated the
word "hate," but I hated him. I remember finally getting away

from him by running up the street and then my sister grabbing me because my legs couldn't move that fast at 2 a.m., and my father was trying to hit us with his car. We ran across the busiest street in Youngstown, and a bar owner allowed us to use the phone to call the police while he protected us.

I couldn't understand back then, how do we go to church almost every day to come home and endure this? I also felt like, if this was what being a Christian was all about I wanted NO parts of it. I had to later learn that this was not the works of a Christian, that God was loving and kind.

Later on in life both of my parents remarried. I have always had a strong sense of discernment; whether or not I listened to it was on me. The new husband that my mother had, there was something about him that didn't sit well. Everyone else had thought he was a great guy, but I just didn't feel the same way. I received a lot of backlash for it. Well, finally, because I was told often I was taking out on him what my father did to us, I decided to be his friend. He clearly took advantage of it and tried to rape me. Luckily, I was able to fight him off, but when I told my family hardly no one believed me. At that time I tried to kill myself, and I wanted to kill him. Instead, I joined everything I could in school and got a job. This allowed me to only be at home at night and then wake up in the morning to go to wherever I had to. I avoided what was supposed to be my safe haven. I avoided going home. That was the time I really needed a real father, but my father still wasn't there. I stopped talking to my family for years. My older sisters moved out to escape the dysfunctional household. Teenage to adult, I then met an older man who became my husband and the father of my two wonderful children. Now that I am older, I realized I was seeking a father when I met him. I had received so many signs to not marry him, and yet I did. The marriage wasn't all bad, but it wasn't where I was supposed to be. I have always known and have been told that I have a calling on my life, but I am still wondering and asking God what it is. I was married at the young age of 19, and I remained married for 10 years until we separated and later divorced. I moved to Florence to save my marriage. I started a restaurant in Lake City, of all places I didn't know. It did great until our marriage didn't. I know our marriage was not ordained by God, but I needed love so bad that I would take it, no matter the cost. I didn't have any family or friends here. Then he went through his own storm, and I didn't see him for four years. Within those four years, I met whom now I consider an angel, which was Officer Carraway. He helped my children and me in every way he could. He helped me find a job, apartment, childcare, etc. Six months after my husband left that is when my daughter became ill. Within three months my daughter was in ICU, and I had lost my job. Thank God, because I had been paying my rent on time up until then, they worked with me. I had lost all my pride that I didn't need anyway. I had a can begging. I did GO FUND ME pages. I asked friends and family for help. I was shocked by the people who didn't help me and shocked by those who did. I felt hopeless. Sometimes I didn't know how I was going to make it. I didn't know how I was going to feed my children or if they would have a roof over their head. During that time I felt so alone. My 10-year-old son at the time would help me rotate shifts staying up with his sick sister. She was sick for 10-12 hours out of a 24-hour day.

This went on for almost two years, traveling to about 16 different hospitals across the U.S. God placed in my life a few great people during this rough time in this strange land I had come to.

I will not mention them all but Tina, Angie, Demetric, Isis, Vashon, Darren, and Isaac, just to name a few. During this time I remember sitting on the couch and receiving a phone call that my stepfather had raped my 10-year-old niece. I felt so guilty because I should have been there to protect her because I knew how he was, although no one believed me. He was suspected to have raped my nephew too. I had prayed, and after the third day of my daughter being sick, God revealed to me what she had, and no one believed me, but finally someone listened. I just hoped it was in enough time because she was now wheelchair bound. She had a genetic condition called Dystonia, and my sister and my daughter were suffering from it. Well, God favored us, and she was able to get out of the wheel chair and walk again!

Then I started My Delivery Doctor to help those who couldn't get out because I needed it when I couldn't get out. Then a year later my daughter was being bullied, and then it was a huge story. This story reached millions. Again, this story is not finished, so it is to be continued. Then Carraway died... then my grandfather and then my aunt... I didn't even really have time to grieve because of dealing with so much other stuff. This has been going on for almost six years. My business has had its ups and downs, my family life too. I then met you, "Bob The Encourager." I guess this is God showing me that He is always here, and He has never left me because, Mr. Bob, I smile a lot, but I am physically, mentally, and spiritually tired. I feel drained and as if life is beating me up. I feel like some days I'm so tired from doing nothing, and I ask God to remove that because I know depression is trying to sneak in. I have learned a lot. I have forgiven my father, and I thank God he has changed. I have forgiven my family for not believing me, and I have forgiven myself. Now I just want to be free. I want to have peace. I want true joy and happiness, and I want to know my purpose.

Please pray for me, Mr. Bob, and thanks for the encouragement.

SLP. I wanted to include this story, to show those who don't have to live like this the importance of BEING AN ENCOUR-AGER people are hurting. Think about this lady, but there is more, and she is becoming the normal in the society we live in today. "Be an Encourager." As we get close to the end, I hope you feel the passion I have for our country!

CHAPTER THIRTEEN

Challenge to Becoming an Encourager

I FIND ACRONYMS to be a great memory device to help me remember deeper meanings. Here's a unique way to look at the word ENCOURAGER because it not only drills deeper into the meaning, but it also challenges you to remember ten specific ideas. These ideas can encourage you personally, especially when you are in a tough corner.

E-Equipped—God always equips those He has called.

N-Never give up—As long as you have breath and a heartbeat, there is hope.

C-Courage—You give others courage when you encourage.

O-Others—When you are an encourager, it takes the focus off you and puts it on thee: "from me to thee."

U-Unity—When you are encouraging others, it draws you closer to people.

R-Relationships—One of the most amazing things that happens from a close relationship with our Heavenly Father is that He can guide us, prepare us, and lead us to accomplish the race He called us to run. God has been trying to re-establish a relationship with man since the Garden of Eden.

A-Attitude—Your attitude as an encourager is not critical of others. You are a delight to be around. Find the good in others, and lift up your neighbor.

G-Genuine—Encouragers are genuinely caring people, not focused on what's in it for them but rather on the one being encouraged. A phony, self-serving "encourager" can be spotted right off the bat.

E-Empower—As you encourage others, you will be empowered and challenged by how you serve others. As a giver, you will be encouraged by what you do for others.

R-Recharge—It is necessary to recharge your spiritual and emotional battery daily. Recharging will keep you from giving up. I believe we are in a battle, and it's going to take all the strength we can muster. It only takes one person to start a movement, but ultimately, it will take millions to achieve the desired results. I need your help to share these ideas and to encourage others to get involved. The word of mouth is still the most effective way to spread a message. This book and the associated website and social media platforms are very low-cost tools designed to serve others. Just like my counsel to read the book quickly, the faster we get this to others, the more we can accelerate the viral impact on America and nations around the globe.

At the time of this writing, our team is talking to a number of people who are promising to support this effort with substantial time and financial investments. At the same time, I know others can help in different ways, primarily by becoming an encourager. The bottom line is that when your heart is on the mission, you will be led to invest time and money in a way that is best for you. As you can imagine, Sue and I have made a very significant time and financial commitment to the project because we are committed to encouraging the people of America and the world. You may consider encouraging your church to support us as a home missions project, which may open up options to access third-party funds. In many cases, this could begin with small donations that buy cases of books to give away in the local community or to share with small groups.

It will take years to complete the first phase of this project, so the need will be huge. The primary focus is to build a strong core leadership team of encouragers.

My role is to be a good steward of this God-sized idea. Fortunately, since I have experienced the tough lessons in the business school of "hard knocks," as well as success, I can apply what I have learned to serve this mission. There is wisdom in a multitude of counselors, so our team will guard ourselves from mistakes by soliciting input and ideas from many others, including you. No idea or comment is too small; that's actually where most of the big ideas start. I really believe the more people who input to the system, the smarter we get. Along the way, we will debrief and ask questions. What did we do right? What did we do wrong, or what do we need to change? I guess I am just wired this way, but I would rather die at doing something big than win at doing something small. I realized a long time ago, if I only give 75 percent in any day, I can't rollover that 25 percent and add it to the next day; it's gone forever. So my goal is to give 100 percent every day.

QUESTIONS TO CONSIDER

Write your own personal definition of the acronym,

E-N-C-O-U-R-A-G-E-R.

E Equipped—

N Never give up—

C Courage—

O Others—

U Unity—

R Relationships—

A Attitude—

G Genuine—

E Empower—

R Recharge—

The Amazing Power Of An Encourager (What Are You Starting To See Happen?)

CHAPTER FOURTEEN

I Love...

THIS PROJECT IS about the God, people, and country I love. This passion of mine has been building for some time now. While traveling around the country working on similar projects, I kept finding they did not address all the areas that I felt needed to be changed to correct our country's course. As I would discuss these ideas, I continually heard the suggestion, "Someone needs to do something." The problem was that nobody ever stepped up to the challenge, which is why it became clear that God called me to do so. Now we are starting to see others get a glimpse of our vision and agree with our plan to change our direction and restore hope in our country. In my heart of hearts, I believe the majority of citizens are looking for a change that will encourage themselves and their families. I am sincerely asking you to join our efforts to make the turn toward a brighter future. I really believe history will agree with us because, from my vantage point, it's clear many people are starting to agree with us, which excites me even more. As this book inspires a grassroots encouragement revolution, I can imagine the proverbial snowball rolling down a hill, picking up speed, and encouraging more and more people. One of the things I love about our plan is that it doesn't discriminate, and at its core, it doesn't require any money. So politicians on both sides of the aisle will have a hard time ignoring it. One of my key intentions is to ask politicians of both parties to unite around this idea of encouragement. Healthy debate in a two-party system can be good for a society, but political strategies designed to divide and conquer are antithetical to our founders' and framers' vision for America. When elected officials focus on division of any kind, everyone loses.

President Gerald Ford said, "Government that is big enough to give you everything you want is more likely to simply take everything you've got."[19]

President Reagan stated, "Our liberty springs from and depends upon an abiding faith in God."[20]

You've heard me say, "To *know* is nothing; to *do* is everything!" I am actively encouraging those who want to be encouraged. In other words, those who actively seek division and strife will not be attracted to our plan.

You must remember, there are the red-light people, and their response to this plan will make it plain to see who they really are. Our plan is to strengthen the weakest link because we want everyone to be a better you. If you choose to reject kindness and encouragement, then you make it impossible to serve others. Are you willing to become an encourager? If you make the choice to become one *(It's all about change)*, you will be the winner; you will become a better you. Finally, I'd like to encourage my fellow Christian brothers and sisters. We must be the people who set an example for others, just as Jesus has done for us. Division within and among churches is one of the primary reasons people on the outside avoid organized religion like the plague. All they see and hear is hypocrisy, gossip, and anything but a path to salvation. Who's responsible for that? It's not the pastor; it's you and me. If we own the responsibility to demonstrate the characteristics of an encourager in our daily lives, people around us will notice. If we choose to assassinate others' character, then we are going to reap what we sow. We cannot be both encouragers and assassins. We must look in the mirror and decide whom we will serve.

As Joshua said many moons ago, "As for me and my house, We will serve the Lord." I would much rather build people up than tear them down. Win-Win is much better than Lose-Lose. At the root of this entire encouragement idea is LOVE.

Here's a short list of the most important loves of my life: What is your order? Is God first and you last? We are born with a nature to love self, but this is where the change is to take place. Now, rearrange the list. If you are not at the bottom, you need to start to work toward this as a goal.

I love my God.
I love myself.
I love my wife.
I love my children.
I love my grandchildren.
I love my friends.
I love my country.

QUESTIONS TO CONSIDER

Have you ever thought deeply about your loves?

1. Will you make a list of the most important loves in your life?

2. As encouragers, we should change the order of whom we love the most.

3. If you truly want to experience Joy. J _____ O _____ You.

4. To be an encourager, who are the others in your life? 1. _____ 2. _____ 3. _____

CHAPTER FIFTEEN

Your Legacy

THE LIFELONG SEARCH for purpose is born in all of us. I have found most people never truly discover their purpose, or they give up the search too early in life. At the time of this writing, I am seventy years old. As I move into the last season of my life, I have been reading, studying, and praying for God to show me clearly what He made me for...my purpose...my legacy. Candidly, I did not want to write this book, but I heard the still, small voice inside me say very clearly, *Write a book.*

"Okay, God, I will write a book." The prompting I felt made it clear to me the book I was to write must encourage people. Check! God does not always call the equipped, *but He always equips the called.*

"Okay, God, what's next? You placed in me a desire to make a difference. Most people want to make a difference." The Lord inspired me to find people whose purpose is to make a difference. God made it crystal clear this is not about me; it's all about you.

The purpose of being an encourager is to make *you a better you.* I am here to serve you. This book has been written to serve you. As you embrace my encouragement and become an encourager to others, people will notice. In their mind, people who observe your encouragement will say to themselves, "I don't know what they have, but I want it. There is just something different about them." You will have become the encourager, focused on taking it from *"me to thee."*

The next step is to build a team that will spread the message of hope throughout our nation. We must restore hope to citizens who are feeling hopeless and who long to see a return of our country to our Founding Fathers' principles. When you join the team and start to practice the role of an encourager, your life will explode with purpose, meaning, and significance, knowing you are making a difference. Wow, **I love** doing something that makes a difference.

Before we conclude, I want to share my personal encouragement to consider pursuing a vertical relationship with our Heavenly Father. It will take vertical encouragement for you to make the horizontal *(horizontal means person to person)* encouragement work with others. Maybe you made a personal commitment to Christ earlier in your life but would like to work on your relationship with daily recharging sessions. I encourage you to start this daily habit because this is the ultimate, eternal source of *The Power of an Encourager*™. If you have questions about this vertical relationship, contact us at this e-mail: *bob@winningamerica.us.* We will have someone contact you, depending on where you live. To help you move from *knowing to doing,* I've developed a free resource called "The Encourager's Daily Planner." This will be delivered to you instantly as soon as you register as an encourager.

This is an amazing journey, and I look forward to working with you and encouraging our nation! Your legacy will largely be determined by those you encourage. I hope and pray you tap into *The Power of an Encourager*™ and inspire others. I believe this is my purpose; I want to join the team and make a difference.

Sign me up._____

Before you sign, let me cover one more area. For most of us to become encouragers, it will require some change of our attitude and actions. This kind of change will not come easy! To become an encourager to others is to work on your horizontal relationships (horizontal means person to person). In my experience, I have learned that to change and become an encourager requires a vertical relationship. This vertical relationship will be your source for the encouragement you need. By vertical encouragement, I mean having a relationship with the God of the Universe, the God of the Bible. This relationship is only possible through trusting in Jesus Christ, the Son of God, as your personal Savior. It comes through trusting in the fact that His death on a cross 2,000 years ago paid for your sins and opened the door for you and me, imperfect people, to have a relationship with a perfect God. Through trusting in what Jesus did and calling out to God in prayer to forgive you and save you, you can become a child of God. This trusting relationship with God not only provides you the encouragement you need to encourage others, but it will also provide you with eternal life! Once you have settled this most important matter, you need to develop that vertical relationship by spending time every day studying the Word of God (the Bible) to increase your wisdom for life and dealing with others. If you are already trusting in Jesus but are not having a "recharging session" daily, I encourage you to start today. This is the **true** source for *The Amazing Power of an Encourager.*

THE AMAZING POWER OF AN ENCOURAGER

Please e-mail us your contact information at *bob@winningamerica.us* so we can encourage you in this journey as we write our legacy together for our country.

Website: www.winningamerica.us

Join Winning America to help us change the direction of our country before it is too late!

Help us all by being a part of ENCOURAGING, BUILDING-UP, UNITING.

We need your financial support as well as you spreading the message.

Become a team leader by starting a team of 10 holding regular meetings to encourage and train others to spread to positive message across America and then the world.

ENDNOTES

1. internet-American Foundation For Suicide Prevention Statistic AFSP's latest data on suicide are taken from the Centers for Disease Control and Prevention (CDC) Data & Statistics Fatal Injury Report for 2017. Suicide rates listed are Age-Adjusted Rates
2. Zig Ziglar's book What I Learned on the way to the Top page 96
3. Zig Ziglar's book What I Learned on the way to the Top page 84
4. internet John Maxwell's Quotes Page 2
5. three of California's Biggest Fires Ever Are Burning Right Now By TIM WALLACE, ASH NGU, DENISE LU and MATTHEW BLOCH 2018 AUG. 10,
6. dictionary.com
7. About one-third of U.S. children are living with an unmarried parent BY GRETCHEN LIVINGSTON http://www. pewresearch. org/fact-tank/2018/04/27/about-one-third-of-u-s-children-are-living-with-an-unmarried-parent

8. internet American Foundation For Suicide Prevention Statistic AFSP's latest data on suicide are taken from the Centers for Disease Control and Prevention (CDC) Data & Statistics Fatal Injury Report for 2017. Suicide rates listed are Age-Adjusted Rates

9. internet—American Foundation For Suicide Prevention Statistic AFSP's latest data on suicide are taken from the Centers for Disease Control and Prevention (CDC) Data & Statistics Fatal Injury Report for 2017. Suicide rates listed are Age-Adjusted Rates.

10. internet Times—Why Suicides Are More Common in Richer Neighborhoods By Josh Sanburn @joshsanburn-Nov. 08, 2012 A new paper from the San Francisco Federal Reserve

11. internet Why The CEO Of Coca-Cola Never Dines Along Commentary-Fortune 500 June 2015

12. internet American Foundation For Suicide Prevention Statistic AFSP's latest data on suicide are taken from the Centers for Disease Control and Prevention (CDC) Data & Statistics Fatal Injury Report for 2017. Suicide rates listed are Age-Adjusted Rates

13. mayo clinic website Stress relief from laughter? It's no joke for full article

14. "Make Your Bed" by Admiral William H. McRaven This speech was delivered as the commencement address to the graduates of The University of Texas at Austin on May 17, 2014.

15. We shall fight on the beaches From Wikipedia, the free encyclopedia

16. internet American Foundation For Suicide Prevention Statistic AFSP's latest data on suicide are taken from the Centers for Disease Control and Prevention (CDC) Data & Statistics Fatal Injury Report for 2017. Suicide rates listed are Age-Adjusted Rates

17. Mental Health America Suicide No suicide attempt should be dismissed or treated lightly! Why Do People Attempt Suicide?

18. Quotes by Babe Ruth

19. Good reads your favorite authors-Gerald R. Ford > Quotes

20. THE SECRET TO RONALD REAGAN'S SUCCESS Bill Federer recounts faith of esteemed president Published: 02/05/2018

The Amazing Power of an Encourager

Winning America
WA
Encourage Buildup Unite

Winning America is a 501(c)(3) non-profit corporation
established for the education of all Americans
who are concerned about the future of this nation
and its effect on the world's spiritual health

"If we lose this country, where will we go?"

—*Bob Skelton, CEO*

ABOUT THE AUTHOR

Bob Skelton was born in Zenith, West Virginia, with his humble start to life. Bob was born in his grandmother's home, and the delivering physician was given two chickens in payment. Humbling would be an understatement. This might bring a chuckle from most of the younger readers today. Readers might even question if this were really true. I can assure you it is. When Bob was five years old, his family relocated to Winston Salem, North Carolina, where Bob went to grade school and high school. After high school, Bob was drafted into the army for two years. Bob spent eighteen months of this time in Okinawa, which is off the east coast of China. After returning home from the military, Bob entered the prosthetic program at Bowman-Grey School of Medicine in Winston Salem for two years and then transferred to Duke Medical Center for two years. With the completing of his schooling and passing the American boards for certification, Bob and Sue then moved to Florence, South Carolina, to begin practicing his profession.

After a couple of years, Bob was contacted by a couple of friends to start a floor covering business, which they did. When the big recession of the late 1970s -1980s hit, Bob nearly lost it all. The school of "hard knocks" didn't get Bob down. He rose from the ashes a smarter, shrewder man.

From the lessons he learned during this difficult time, Bob was able to build a highly successful medical business, flying to larger cities and making his state-of-art services timelier for the patients. This different way of doing business made it necessary for Bob to get more pilot training by getting his Multi-Engine Instrument rating.

While acting as pilot, Bob has now accumulated total time in excess of 3,600 hours. Bob was able to purchase one single-engine and three twin-engine aircrafts. This also opened up many doors to use his flying skills to fly physician friends, NASCAR drivers, governors, and Lt. governors. It also allowed Bob's family to travel almost weekly. Bob has served on the Florence Airport Authority for eleven years, as chairman of the Florence Airport Authority for two years, and on other financial boards at his church and property ownership. Bob and his wife, Sue, were married in 1974. On occasion, they enjoy letting other pilots handle the flying duties as they travel around the world to unique destinations. They have been privileged to visit their son, Grant; daughter-in-law, Rebecca; and three grandchildren, Harrison, Suzanne, and Adelle in Hong Kong, vacation in Hawaii, and tour Europe. I would think this has been a pretty exciting life for Bob, a little two-chicken baby from Zenith, West Virginia. Bob, a.k.a. "two-chicken baby," has come a long way and led a pretty exciting life since his early days in West Virginia. Now, in his sunset years, Bob is focused on sharing *The Amazing Power of an Encourager*™ with you so you can receive the immense joy that has helped him throughout his entire life.

Most importantly, Bob wants you to share *"The Amazing Power of an Encourager" TM* with others so they can experience the blessing of encouragements from someone who truly cares. I want to invite you to be a part of the team in making a difference by allowing us to send updates and news so you are well informed next.

www.ingramcontent.com/pod-product-compliance
Lightning Source LLC
Chambersburg PA
CBHW021647120626
46545CB00002B/748